CHINA'S REPATRIATION OF NORTH KOREAN REFUGEES

HEARING

BEFORE THE

CONGRESSIONAL-EXECUTIVE COMMISSION ON CHINA

ONE HUNDRED TWELFTH CONGRESS

SECOND SESSION

MARCH 5, 2012

Printed for the use of the Congressional-Executive Commission on China

Available via the World Wide Web: http://www.cecc.gov

U.S. GOVERNMENT PRINTING OFFICE

74–809 PDF   WASHINGTON : 2012

For sale by the Superintendent of Documents, U.S. Government Printing Office
Internet: bookstore.gpo.gov   Phone: toll free (866) 512–1800; DC area (202) 512–1800
Fax: (202) 512–2104   Mail: Stop IDCC, Washington, DC 20402–0001

CONGRESSIONAL-EXECUTIVE COMMISSION ON CHINA

LEGISLATIVE BRANCH COMMISSIONERS

House

CHRISTOPHER H. SMITH, New Jersey, *Chairman*
FRANK WOLF, Virginia
DONALD A. MANZULLO, Illinois
EDWARD R. ROYCE, California
TIM WALZ, Minnesota
MARCY KAPTUR, Ohio
MICHAEL HONDA, California

Senate

SHERROD BROWN, Ohio, *Cochairman*
MAX BAUCUS, Montana
CARL LEVIN, Michigan
DIANNE FEINSTEIN, California
JEFF MERKLEY, Oregon
SUSAN COLLINS, Maine
JAMES RISCH, Idaho

EXECUTIVE BRANCH COMMISSIONERS

SETH D. HARRIS, Department of Labor
MARIA OTERO, Department of State
FRANCISCO J. SANCHEZ, Department of Commerce
KURT M. CAMPBELL, Department of State
NISHA DESAI BISWAL, U.S. Agency for International Development

PAUL B. PROTIC, *Staff Director*
LAWRENCE T. LIU, *Deputy Staff Director*

(II)

CONTENTS

CHINA'S REPATRIATION OF NORTH KOREAN REFUGEES

MONDAY, MARCH 5, 2012

CONGRESSIONAL-EXECUTIVE
COMMISSION ON CHINA,
Washington, DC.

The hearing was convened, pursuant to notice, at 2:37 p.m., in room 2118, Rayburn House Office Building, Representative Chris Smith, Chairman, presiding.

Also present: Representative Edward R. Royce.

OPENING STATEMENT HON. CHRIS SMITH, A U.S. REPRESENTATIVE FROM NEW JERSEY; CHAIRMAN, CONGRESSIONAL–EXECUTIVE COMMISSION ON CHINA

Chairman SMITH. The Commission will come to order. Thank you all for being here, and good afternoon.

Dozens of North Koreans are today at imminent risk of persecution, torture—even execution—owing to China's decision to forcibly repatriate them in stark violation of both the spirit and the letter of the 1951 Refugee Convention and the 1967 Protocol to which China has acceded.

The international community—especially the United Nations, the Obama administration, and the U.S. Congress—must insist that China, at long last, honor its treaty obligations, end its egregious practice of systematic refoulement, or be exposed as hypocrites.

Article 33 of the Convention and Protocol Relating to the Status of Refugees couldn't be more clear:

> Prohibition of Expulsion or Return ("Refoulement"): No Contracting State shall expel or return ("refouler") a refugee in any manner whatsoever to the frontiers of territories where his life or freedom would be threatened on account of race, religion, nationality, membership of a particular social group or political opinion.

Today's hearing underscores an emergency that begs an immediate remedy. Lives are at risk. The North Korean refugees—disproportionately women—face death or severe sexual abuse and torture unless they get immediate protection. China has a duty to protect.

In recent weeks we have learned that Chinese authorities have reportedly detained dozens—perhaps as many or more than 40— North Korean refugees. North Korea's leader, Kim Jong-un, has threatened to "exterminate three generations" of any family with a member caught defecting from North Korea during the 100-day mourning period for the late Kim Jong-il. Frankly, I believe him.

It is unclear whether or not the Obama administration's food aid to North Korea—some 240,000 metric tons per year—contains any conditions or links to the refugees. It should.

Forced repatriation by China of North Koreans, as we all know, isn't new. But that doesn't make what is about to happen to dozens of new victims any less offensive. According to testimony submitted today by Roberta Cohen, chair of the Committee for Human Rights in North Korea and a non-resident Senior Fellow at The Brookings Institution:

> China has forcibly returned tens of thousands over the past two decades. Most, if not all, have been punished in North Korea. According to testimonies and reports received by the Committee for Human Rights, the punishment has included beatings, torture, detention, forced labor, sexual violence, and in the case of women suspected of becoming pregnant in China, forced abortions or infanticide.

For the record, I would note that since 2005, I have chaired four congressional hearings that focused in whole or in part on the plight of North Korean refugees and China's ongoing violations of international law.

The Chinese Government claims that North Korean refugees are illegal economic migrants, not refugees. Furthermore, the Chinese Government continues its policy of repatriating North Koreans in China according to a bilateral repatriation agreement that requires it to return all border crossers.

As we will hear today, in doing so, China is in clear violation of its obligations of international law. Again, these are obligations that it freely entered into. Under international law and standards, these detained refugees are entitled to protection if there is a well-founded reason to believe that they will be persecuted upon return. There are documented accounts, as well as strong evidence. We know that the persecution exists and what awaits them if they are forced to return.

North Korea is certainly at fault. It might also be stated that China has contributed to the humanitarian crisis through its policy of gendercide, the killing of baby girls by forced abortion, or infanticide. China's one-child-per-couple policy has led to the worst gender disparity in any nation in history, and that is directly connected to the issue that we probe today.

According to the 2011 Commission's report, NGOs and researchers estimate that as many as 70 percent of the North Korean refugees in China are women, and some researchers have estimated that 9 out of every 10 North Korean women in China are trafficked, usually into sex trafficking.

In the past we have heard in my subcommittee from women who had been forced into trafficking. In one case we heard from a woman whose daughter crossed the border and then she and her daughter went looking for the missing daughter and sister, only to be forced into sex trafficking themselves. They testified before our committee and told of their harrowing experience and the courage that they had to overcome it.

The Chinese Government needs to change and the time has come now for us to clearly and unambiguously raise the stakes. It is time for a change.

Our focus today is on China's role and responsibility in solving this problem. At this time we call on China to uphold its international obligations and take immediate steps to end this cruel, barbaric policy of sending North Koreans back to persecution or death.

China must conform to international norms and allow these refugees safe passage to the Republic of Korea, or grant them immediate asylum. And we ask the Chinese Government to take all steps necessary to meet the requirements of the convention relating to the status of refugees and its protocol.

And the United Nations. It is time for the United Nations to step up and stop writing just short comments and commentaries on this, and its leaders, including the head of the UN High Commissioner for Refugees [UNHCR] and others, need to speak boldly about what is about to happen to these refugees.

Finally, I want to thank all of our witnesses for being here at this emergency hearing. It is a special honor to welcome Ms. Han Songhwa and her daughter, Jo Jinhye, former North Korean refugees who are here to share their personal accounts of detention, hardship, and loss. I am sure that their reflections and observations will deepen our understanding of this issue and strengthen our resolve that China must immediately address this self-made crisis.

I would like to yield to my good friend and colleague, Representative Royce, for any comments he might have.

STATEMENT OF HON. EDWARD R. ROYCE, A U.S. REPRESENTATIVE FROM CALIFORNIA; MEMBER, CONGRESSIONAL–EXECUTIVE COMMISSION ON CHINA

Representative ROYCE. Thank you very much, Chairman Smith. Thank you for holding this hearing.

This is an emergency. The Chinese Government is set to repatriate many North Korean refugees, so there is an urgency to this hearing. There is an urgency to Congress acting. We are, for those of us who have been in North Korea, as I have, or who have interviewed those who have survived coming over the border and being repatriated or have had family members—I remember talking, speaking with one young woman whose brother attempted to cross with her and he was caught. He died by firing squad.

Speaking to Hwang Jang Yop, who was the Propaganda Minister from North Korea, he told us the stories about the administration in North Korea making the decision that they would not allow food to go to the "No Go" areas; that close to 2 million people had starved to death because the North Korean regime wanted to build up its nuclear program, its ICBM [intercontinental ballistic missile] program, and made a calculated decision to allow people to starve and felt that people in those areas could not be depended upon, they were suspect in those regions. So they allowed them to starve to death.

You have reports by the State Department and NGOs that we are going to study today that show a very grim picture of what is happening in North Korea, a total denial of political and civil and religious liberties. We know that. But the severe physical abuse that is visited on those who are simply suspected or accused of not being in step with the regime, anyone who is accused of violating a restriction or a law—you have a system of concentration camps akin to the Soviet Gulag system.

The photographs I have seen are very reminiscent to the ones taken in Nazi Germany. You have 200,000 people in these camps, most of them with no hope of ever getting out. There are a few who have managed to get out, to escape over into China. We have interviewed them about the conditions, and they are horrifying.

So this dismal state has led to a large number of North Koreans, particularly women, trying to escape to take their children out of this environment, perhaps as many as 300,000. They have fled into China and there they seek food or work and resettlement to South Korea. Seventy-five percent of these refugees are women. Up to 90 percent, according to some sources, end up being trafficked.

In northeast China, North Korean refugees live in constant fear of being rounded up by Chinese authorities. Why is that? It's because, despite its international obligations, China does not follow that international law and it forcibly repatriates North Korean refugees. This, for many, is effectively a death sentence.

Why is that so? Because leaving North Korea is considered a crime by the regime and it is punishable by execution or being worked to death in the Gulag. There are new reports that Kim Jung-Eun has issued a "shoot to kill" order to North Korean guards patrolling the border, another reason why this hearing is important today.

Sadly, thousands—thousands—of North Korean children have been abandoned or orphaned in the Chinese countryside. They are threatened by starvation and disease. That is why I introduced H.R. 1464, which calls on the Secretary of State to develop a strategy to facilitate the adoption of North Korean children by U.S. citizens. Many here have supported this legislation.

China's mistreatment of refugees is not new. What is new today is the intensity. As part of its stepped up repatriation campaign, Chinese authorities have established detention centers along the border with North Korea to accommodate greater numbers of North Koreans being held there.

This is what I want to tell you about, because those associated with humanitarian groups who assist North Korean refugees are also being targeted at this time by these Chinese officials. And by the way, that includes U.S. citizens. There is one in particular that I know who was held in one of these facilities; we worked to get him out.

American businessman Steve Kim is another example of a man who spent four years in prison, and his supposed crime was helping North Korean refugees who had escaped their homeland and were hiding in China. They hoped to make their way to South Korea. And remember, this is the international agreement that China is under, to assist in helping those people escape.

But Mr. Kim recounted here on Capitol Hill, "When I was in prison I saw North Korean defectors who I shared the prison cell with beaten to a pulp by prison guards." That was before they were sent back to North Korea. That is the conditions that exist in China.

The human rights situation there, there is only one word for it: It is a nightmare. It demands the international community getting engaged to reverse this, and these human rights abuses demand our attention here in Congress. I thank the Commission for holding this timely hearing.

Chairman SMITH. Thank you very much, Mr. Royce.

I would like to now welcome our first very distinguished panel, beginning with Suzanne Scholte, who is president of the Defense Forum Foundation. Ms. Scholte hosted the first North Korean defectors ever to speak out in the United States back in 1997, and since that time has hosted over 70 visits of defectors, from high-ranking officials to survivors of the North Korean political prison camps and victims of human trafficking in China. She is also the chairwoman of the North Korea Freedom Coalition and vice chair of the Committee for Human Rights in North Korea.

We will then hear from Ms. Songhwa Han, who escaped to China in the mid-1990s and later returned through North Korea, where she was imprisoned and tortured. She escaped to China again several years later with her children.

While living as a refugee in China she encountered forced marriage, domestic abuse, forced labor, detention, official beatings, and eventual repatriation. Ms. Han received protection with the UNHCR in 2006 and asylum in the United States in 2008.

We will then hear from Ms. Jinhye Jo, Ms. Han's daughter, a former North Korean refugee detained in China, repatriated to North Korea and detained in North Korea. Jo received protection with the UNHCR in 2006 and asylum in the United States in 2008. Since arriving in the United States she has been an active advocate on behalf of other North Korean refugees still living in China.

Ms. Scholte, if you could begin.

STATEMENT OF SUZANNE SCHOLTE, PRESIDENT, DEFENSE FORUM FOUNDATION; CHAIRMAN AND FOUNDING MEMBER, NORTH KOREA FREEDOM COALITION

Ms. SCHOLTE. Congressman Smith, Congressman Royce, I want to thank you deeply for responding to this urgent crisis facing North Korean refugees in China today.

Congressman Smith, in September you hosted a hearing with North Korean defector Kim Hye-sook, who is the longest-serving survivor of the North Korean political prisoner camps. She spent 28 years in Bukchang Political Prison Camp.

I mention her today because the reason she was sent to jail at the age of 13, with her entire family, and sent to Bukchang where her brother and sister are still being imprisoned, was simply because her grandfather allegedly had escaped to South Korea. She is a living example of how the regime retaliates against three generations of a family if just one family member flees North Korea.

As draconian as these measures have been, the current situation is even more critical for the North Korean refugees recently arrested in China. Most face execution for three reasons. First of all, Kim Jong-un, as you mentioned, announced in December that the entire family and relatives should be annihilated if any family member fled during the 100-day mourning period following Kim Jong-il's death.

Second, among the group of North Koreans arrested in February are refugees who have family members who defected to South Korea. In fact, the parents of a 19-year-old girl arrested in China have pleaded that their daughter be allowed to commit suicide rather than be repatriated back to North Korea. There is also a 71-year-old mother who has a daughter in South Korea, a 16-year-old whose brother is in South Korea, and a mother and an infant. These refugees are trying desperately to be reunited with their family in South Korea.

Third, China is providing information to North Korea about the refugees it has arrested, informing the North Korea security agents if they were trying to flee to South Korea. Because of this collusion the Chinese Government is complicit in premeditated murder because it knows that these refugees, when repatriated to North Korea, face execution.

By refusing to honor its international treaty commitments and colluding with North Korea to repatriate these refugees, China has created a violent environment where 80 percent of North Korean females are subjected to human trafficking and North Korean agents are allowed to freely roam around China, assassinating humanitarian workers and hunting down refugees.

The Chinese Government wants to be seen as a responsible international leader, yet it refuses to allow the UNHCR access to these refugees, but has no problem allowing North Korean spies and assassins free reign. This collusion with North Korea proves most definitely that China cannot hide behind its claim that these refugees are economic migrants.

As China knows full well and has known for decades, when they force North Koreans back to North Korea they face certain torture, certain imprisonment, and increasingly, execution for fleeing their homeland. China has decided that they should be executed rather than reunited with their families.

According to Kim Sung-min of Free North Korea Radio, China began separating North Korean defectors into two groups based on whether they were trying to escape to South Korea, starting in at least 2008. We suspect this was part of the crackdown before the Beijing Olympics, as China greatly feared that the world would come to know about their cruel treatment of North Korean refugees.

North Korean defectors Ju Seong-ha, a reporter with Dong-a Ilbo, and Kim Yong-hwa, have described how China uses a different-colored stamp on the interrogation papers for those refugees attempting to get to South Korea, the information it provides to North Korea when the refugees are repatriated. China is literally marking these refugees for death.

We need to convince China that it is in their best interests to reverse their repatriation policy and work with the international community to resolve this crisis. In fact, China's action is not only causing this refugee crisis, but prolonging it.

Here is why: China fears an increasing flow of refugees, if it allows refugees safe passage to South Korea, but China's actions are ensuring that there will always be refugees by relieving Kim Jong-un of taking any measures that would improve conditions in North Korea. North Koreans are fleeing North Korea out of desperation.

They know the considerable risk they are taking and most North Koreans who have fled desire to return to North Korea once conditions improve. China has long desired that the Kim regime adopt reform. By forcibly sending fleeing North Koreans back to North Korea, China relieves any pressure for Kim to improve conditions in North Korea so the citizens do not want to flee.

Second, China's future will be much better toward people if it works with South Korea rather than kowtowing to this dictator in North Korea. The two countries celebrate the 20th anniversary of their diplomatic ties this year and enjoy a robust trade relationship. South Korean culture is very popular in China, and many Chinese tourists travel to South Korea. Working with South Korea on this issue will have a positive benefit to their future relationship because it is inevitable that Korea one day will be unified.

Third, all the remedies for resolving this issue are immediately at hand to ensure no burden on China, including the presence of the UNHCR in Beijing; a humanitarian network, and a strong commitment from South Korea and the United States to help resettle refugees.

Finally, China needs to be reminded of what this regime really thinks of the Chinese people. Kim Jong-il had a long-established policy known as "Block the Yellow Wind," as he was resistant to adopting any China-style reforms.

His racist contempt for the Chinese people was evident when he ordered his border guards to beat the bellies of pregnant North Korean females who had been repatriated because their unborn babies were half Chinese. This is a perfect opportunity for China to work with the international community rather than kowtow to a brutal dictatorship, frequently cited as one of the world's worst regimes.

I want to close by recognizing one of your colleagues, Assemblywoman Park Sun-young of the Korean National Assembly, who began a hunger strike in Seoul, calling for China not to repatriate these refugees but allow them safe passage to South Korea. This brave woman collapsed on Friday and was rushed to the hospital. We urge all parliamentarians and governments around the world to join her in calling upon China to end their brutal repatriation policy and stop sending North Koreans to their death.

Thank you, Mr. Chairman.

Chairman SMITH. Ms. Scholte, thank you very much for your eloquent statement and for your ongoing and absolutely tenacious advocacy on behalf of North Korean human rights in general, and refugees in particular. So, thank you so very much.

I would like to now ask Ms. Han if she would present her testimony to the Commission.

STATEMENT OF SONGHWA HAN, FORMER NORTH KOREAN REFUGEE DETAINED IN CHINA, REPATRIATED TO NORTH KOREA, AND DETAINED IN NORTH KOREA

Ms. HAN. Hello, my name is Songhwa Han, and I came to the United States with my two daughters in 2008 as refugees, following the passage of the North Korean Human Rights Act by the U.S. Congress in 2004.

For the lowest class people in North Korea, they have a most desperate and earnest plea. That plea is to be freed and liberated to freedom and human rights from the worst suffering and pain of starvation.

I want to thank the U.S. Government for hearing our plea, for hope, and giving us freedom. I want to just describe very briefly my reasons for leaving North Korea.

I escaped with my two daughters from North Korea for the first time in 1998. Before defection from North Korea, my family consisted of eight people. My mother and my two-month-old newborn baby son died from starvation, and my oldest daughter, who was 18 years old at the time, left home to find food and never came back. To this day I do not know of her whereabouts or what happened to her.

I had another five-year-old son who I had to leave at an acquaintance's home before I escaped to China. I promised my son, if you just sleep for five nights I will be back with rice and candy and I will come back to get you.

Afterward, my five-year-old son, who was suffering from malnutrition, was kicked out of the house I had put him in and died while waiting and crying out, "Mommy, sister, when are you coming back?" He cried and cried, and died in a grass field. This news was delivered to me by someone I had hired to go and bring my son to China.

My husband was arrested and sent to jail for the crime of crossing the Tumen River and going to China and bringing back a sack of rice, when what he had done was simply to go to China to find food for his children and save them, who had slowly over time grown weaker and weaker from starvation. He died while incarcerated in prison from the severe punishment he received.

Afterward, my family was labeled as anti-state traitors for having crossed over to China and the North Korean police and the Bowibu, or the national or domestic security agents, came to look for us in our countryside village home. They came to kick us out of the village, for me to take the remaining family members and move away to another place.

Our family had devoted ourselves to the Party and to the dear leader, but contrary to the police in the United States, instead of protecting the citizens the North Korean police yelled and threatened to burn down our house if we did not move out.

I could no longer beg for help or for mercy, and I decided right then and there rather than staying put and starve to death, even if we died trying to go find our way to freedom, I decided to seek out freedom.

My one sole wish was to feed my children just one meal of white rice, and decided that I would never suffer from starvation or be unfairly mistreated, and therefore took my seven-year-old daughter, who was malnourished and was not growing up properly, put her in a sack and carried her, and held my older daughter's hand and leaned on one another and each other and crossed the waist-high currents of the Tumen River and safely escaped from North Korea.

After escaping to China and living in fear for almost 10 years, during that period we were forcibly repatriated four times. During one of those forced repatriations, I would just like to share about my experience from the time I was forcibly repatriated during the summer of 2003.

First of all, once a North Korean defector was handed over by the Chinese police to the North Korean Bowibu, or the security agents, one had to become an animal.

Second, the defectors were repatriated or ordered by the North Korean guards that, "You are all dogs from now on, so therefore lower your head and move around by only looking at the ground." The prisoners are handcuffed and chained to one another, and if the slightest noise is made the prisoners are beaten with rifle butts.

After the interrogation is finished at the Bowibu, the prisoners are taken to a reformed hard labor camp, where I was sent. We were forced to work from 5 o'clock in the morning until late at night, and after dragging our dead-tired bodies back from work we were only giving a fist-sized corn/rice ball to eat, and until 11 o'clock in the evening we were required to participate in self-reflection and self-criticism group meetings and forced to sing patriotic martial songs.

We would then spend the rest of our night sitting in front of one another and picking off the ticks and lice from our clothes and our hair, and then sleep for a few hours, and then wake up early in the morning to the wake-up call and then get dragged out for more labor. These types of punishments were given out to misdemeanor criminals.

These punishments were repeated for as long as six months, and like men who would die from malnutrition and starvation and the women prisoners who collapsed from fatigue and could not get up again, both women and men alike had to carry heavy logs up to the mountainside. If a prisoner became injured there was no recourse for medicine or for medical care.

In the wintertime there was no proper footwear available, so pieces of cloth and strings would be used to cover up the feet. While working in the snow, many would come down with frostbite, but we could not stop work and had to continue working, and also continue to work the following day.

Sometimes the men had to shovel human waste from the latrines with their own bare hands. The women prisoners would then carry the human waste, mixed with dirt, on their backs and carry the load into the fields. So for the crime of going to China for only wanting to live and not die from starvation, North Korean refugees who are repatriated by China become prisoners and end up suffering under crushing labor, doing construction work or coal mining work, and become sick or injured, or worse, suffer in misery and pain and die while working under horrendous conditions. The wretched and poor North Korean refugees continue to suffer like this, and the misery is never ending.

For the crime of betraying the nation, in the Bowibu, the domestic or national security agency prisons, the North Korean refugee men who were forcibly repatriated were beaten with steel pipes and countless people died from beatings inflicted on them, where arms and legs were broken.

I, myself, was beaten in the head for the crime of having gone over to China, and I was beaten so severely that my skull still has pieces of bone imbedded in my head. Besides this injury, because I was beaten so severely and punched around so much, my eyes became swollen and one of my eardrums ruptured. To this day I am hard of hearing in one ear.

While we were suffering from thirst, there was no water to drink and the prisoners would end up drinking foul water from the water tanks or wells and come down with colitis, and die without any care or treatment given to them.

North Korean refugees, if they are miraculously able to survive and be released from prison or from the reform labor camps, will attempt to escape from North Korea even if it means death if caught again.

Through this hearing today I earnestly plead and beg of you, refugees of other countries have been accepted in the United States numbering in the tens of thousands of people or more. But after the North Korean Human Rights Act passed in 2004, only about 130 North Korean refugees have been granted asylum in the United States.

These defectors, who have been separated from their parents, separated from their children, these defectors who have no place to go, these North Korean refugees who are shuddering in fear in China right now and desiring freedom in the free world, whether it be South Korea or the United States, desire to be rescued and accepted into freedom.

If 100 North Korean refugees were accepted after the Human Rights Act passed we would have more than 1,000 North Korean refugees in the United States by now. Those who long to go to the United States and who travel to Thailand and were incarcerated in the detention camps in Thailand, who long to go to the United States, because the wait period was so long, waiting for many months, they decided to change their destination to South Korea and ended up going to South Korea instead.

I sincerely hope that the United States will accept the North Korean refugees, like South Korea. Being accepted into the United States is the wish of many North Korean refugees in earnest, and on their behalf I make this request to all of you here today.

I pray that for those North Korean refugees who are in the period of uncertainty, that you will deal with China intensely and help rescue the North Korean refugees in China right now. Please help us, the North Korean refugees. Thank you.

Chairman SMITH. Ms. Han, thank you very much for your testimony. You and your daughter are surely not just victims and survivors, but you are women of courage who bring a message to Washington and to the world that it must hear. You talked about the misery being never ending. You talked about the unspeakable cruelty. The whole world needs to hear your message. So, I thank you so very much for your being here today and bravely offering your commentary.

I would like to now ask Ms. Jo if she would present her testimony.

STATEMENT OF JINHYE JO, FORMER NORTH KOREAN REFUGEE DETAINED IN CHINA, REPATRIATED TO NORTH KOREA, AND DETAINED IN NORTH KOREA

Ms. Jo. Hello. My name is Jinhye Jo, and I am a North Korean defector. I want to first extend my greeting and deep appreciation to God, the U.S. Government, and the American people for allowing me the freedom to speak before you at this place, and also for the fact that I live in America, a place which is like heaven to me.

In North Korea, one cannot dream of going to Pyongyang freely unless you were a part of the inner circle of Kim Jong-il. However, I am now living in the Washington, DC area, the capital of the United States, and I am here today to make an earnest request.

With the desire to fill our hungry stomachs, we escaped to China to seek the freedom that my mother spoke of. However, what awaited us were the Chinese police and the security officials who were obsessed with searching for, and arresting, North Korean defectors and human traffickers who did not see a mother of two daughters, but rather a source of money-making.

My younger sister and I were young and naive, and were just so glad to be able to eat white rice for a meal. But we always lived in fear, that one morning when we woke up our mother would be taken somewhere to be sold or that she would abandon us and leave us.

By chance, I happened to find God and became a Christian at a small countryside church, and through the grace of God and His protection, even though I was forcibly repatriated four times to North Korea, I did not die from beatings, I did not die from starvation, and I was able to survive and live.

The North Korean Bowibu, or national security agency, officials strip-search the defector women who are sent back, searching every article of clothing to look for hidden money or contraband. If nothing of value is found among the clothing, the prisoners who are standing are told to put their hands on their head and forced to sit and stand up repeatedly until they collapse from exhaustion. If they do collapse, they are relentlessly slapped.

An elderly grandmother who was 65 years old and next to me in the interrogation cells said she could not move any further and she was immediately and mercilessly slapped and beaten, while another young girl and I had our heads bashed against the wall repeatedly.

After the interrogation was over and while in transit to the prison cells, one of the prisoners had talked back to the security guard and we were then mercilessly kicked by the guard, who was wearing boots. We were placed in cells that were crawling with insects and, while trying to sleep at night, because the space was so limited, we literally had to sleep on top of other prisoners.

As a woman, it is hard for me to describe what I saw and experienced, but I want to speak out today with courage for the countless North Korean refugees who have suffered under North Korea's evil and its violation of human rights. North Korean refugees swallow money wrapped in plastic when escaping to China.

During arrest by the Chinese authorities and forced repatriation to North Korea and then going to prison, the money that is expelled naturally is peeled of its soiled plastic and swallowed again.

Another way of hiding money for women is to hide the money in the womb or in the anal cavity.

There was an incident at the Bowibu facility in the Sinuiju in North Korea where a 16-year-old girl's hymen ruptured and she was hemorrhaging blood. The Bowibu agent used a rubber glove used in washing clothes to check for money or contraband in her vagina, and due to the reckless searching the agent had ruptured her hymen.

In their quest to search for money and to rob the prisoners they stopped at nothing, using all kinds of methods and means to do so. A lot of the women prisoners also attempted to give the money they took pains to hide to the security agents with the hope of being shown leniency or being let go.

I remember vividly what happened to a North Korean refugee woman with a baby conceived with a Chinese man, who was repatriated. The head Bowibu security agent cussed profanities at her, yelling at this woman that she was someone who carried a Chinese seed. He then proceeded to torture and beat her with steel hooks by hitting her on the side of the head and forcing her to sit and stand repeatedly for 500 times, until she collapsed.

North Korean agents continued to pour out obscenities such as "dirty bitch" at the woman lying on the floor, and after they picked her up and sat her down on the floor the agents then beat her in the head with a wooden block and caused her nose to bleed and her blood from the beatings splattered all around her in the interrogation room. I saw this with my own eyes. This is one example.

There were situations where we were bitten by bugs and we suffered from inflammation. When the temperatures got so cold and some prisoners were crying out in pain from frostbite, the security guards would punish everyone in the cell.

When my family was repatriated for the last time my mother was hauled to be beaten and tortured. Hearing our mother's blood-curdling screams, my sister and I froze instantly with fear as if our hearts stopped. The head Bowibu agent began to torment and scare us by saying that if we told the truth our mother would not be hit.

Despite this, we did not dare open our mouths. He grabbed our heads by our hair and began hitting us. The pain that was inflicted on us was so bad, we could not lay our heads down properly to sleep for about two weeks.

Another form of punishment and torture I received in the interrogation room was where I was forced to kneel down and a wooden plank was placed between my thighs and between my bent legs. Every time I answered "no" to a question I was kicked, and that would cause me to bowl over. The plank that was placed was tremendously painful, and this was the one way that I was tortured and beaten.

Other forms of beating and torture that I received after being forcibly repatriated by the Chinese authorities, were in one instance, where I was forced to stand on tip-toes and then mercilessly kicked and beaten, kicked and beaten to unconsciousness while forced to kneel, and then the security agents would wake me up with water splashed from an ashtray.

All these methods of severe and cruel punishment were to try to find out whether the North Korean refugees had attempted to eventually escape to South Korea or whether we had attended church or come into contact with Christians while in China.

Our family, I believe, was miraculously saved through God's special grace and mercy. I also believe that God saved me so that I would be able to tell the world the plight of the North Korean people's unfair suffering and the worst modern-day evil that is going on right now.

When I think of the almost three-dozen North Korean refugees who will be experiencing torture and fear on a far worse scale than what I went through, I am filled with dread and fear and my heart aches so much. The North Korean regime, under Kim Jong-un, has declared that any North Korean that attempts to escape during the mourning period for Kim Jong-il will be dealt with most severely, and these refugees who have embarrassed the regime and sought the world's attention to save them will surely be punished to three generations and be given the harshest sentence if they are repatriated by China.

I sincerely and earnestly request that all of you here today, and for those throughout the world who will hear this hearing, that the good fortune and privilege we have now of living in freedom will become a reality for those more than 30 North Korean refugees currently being held by China, only through your combined attention and effort.

I sincerely and earnestly request that you will help save the precious lives of the more than 30 North Korean refugees, lives that are more precious than anything in this world, through talking with the government of China, the government that, even as they are pushing down people who are drowning, reaching out their hands to be rescued.

In the United States alone, over 100,000 people have signed a petition on behalf of saving these 30 North Korean refugees. I know that, because of the attention of this petition, they are not alone. I never had any idea that the people that we were brainwashed and taught to hate as sworn enemies, Americans such as Suzanne Scholte and the distinguished people sitting before me, that I would be sitting here before you and speaking before you today.

I sincerely wish that the fear and terror that they are feeling, which is what I am feeling also, will be felt together as well by all of you, all of us here, and I sincerely and earnestly pray that God will help them. This stack of paper here is the petition signed by the people for the refugees that have been arrested in China recently.

Thank you.

Chairman SMITH. Ms. Jo, thank you so much for your testimony. You have laid out again, like your mom, information that the Congress, the Obama administration, the United Nations, any country that recognizes and prizes human rights and international law cannot ignore—torture, blood-curdling screams from your mother, fists, logs being used in beatings.

Yet, you conclude by saying, "Our family, I believe, was miraculously saved through God's special grace and mercy. I also believe that God saved me so that I would be able to tell the world the plight of the North Korean people's unfair suffering and the worst modern-day evil that is going on right now."

What a tremendous witness, that all people hear this, that the President of the United States hears what you have said so eloquently today. So, thank you so much for providing that witness to this Commission. We hope to amplify your message and to take very bold action ourselves.

Before I get to some questions I would like to yield to my good friend and colleague, Mr. Royce, who does have to leave, for any statements or questions he might have.

Representative ROYCE. Thank you. I would like, Mr. Chairman, to ask a question of Suzanne Scholte. During the horror of the Third Reich, at the waning days of that war when Dachau was liberated, my father had his brother's camera and he took photographs there of the bodies stacked like cord wood next to the ovens where they were being burned, the people starved to death in the box cars. The photographs, by the way, of the prisoners, the uniforms, are almost identical. The striped uniforms, the uniforms you see, these children that are taken that are held in these work camps in North Korea.

Here is the question my father asked me recently. He said, inasmuch as presumably we did not have the intelligence on what was going on as 6 million people were liquidated in these concentration camps, presuming that was the case, we had some excuse for not knowing what we were walking into.

But how does the world today live with its conscience that we have the evidence that this is going on as we speak, that we have the defectors, the survivors, and yet when we say never again to this kind of conduct the international community does not speak with one voice to put the kind of pressure on this and elevate this to the level that the North Koreans are forced to deal with it. Could I ask you that question? What's your thought?

Ms. SCHOLTE. It is an excellent question, a very hard one to answer. But I will try to do that. I think that having been involved in this issue for some time, when we first started bringing defectors from North Korea to testify in the United States, in 1996, people did not believe it. It is much like what happened—in the 1940s— when people were trying to say, "This is what the Nazis are doing right now to the Jewish people." People were like, "There is no way, I can't believe that."

But now we have 23,000 eyewitnesses. They tell the same story. I think the challenge has been, first of all, our reliance on being able to see things first-hand. The reporters, Laura Ling and Euna Lee, are an example. These two reporters went to China to try to record what was happening to North Korean women. North Korean women are being bought and sold right now in China. They went to tell the story, and you know what happened to them. They ended up in Pyongyang.

Representative ROYCE. I worked long and hard to try to assist the two of them.

Ms. SCHOLTE. Yes. But I think that——

Representative ROYCE. And they were American citizens and you saw what they went through.

Ms. SCHOLTE. Exactly. So I think part of the challenge is being able to see the political prison camps. That is why the work of the Committee for Human Rights in North Korea is so important, because they have documented this from survivors. They have showed it. But we only have satellite images. No reporters have been inside a political prison camp. That is always the challenge that we have with the media trying to cover things. Also, the problem also is——

Representative ROYCE. But it is not that difficult. I mean, Mr. Shin—you can see the burns on his body. You can see the scars, the horrific scars. There is no operation that would ever inflict the kinds of things that you and I have seen on the defectors we have interviewed.

Ms. SCHOLTE. No, you are exactly right. That is why what we have done is bring the—we cannot go to the political prison camp and we can't go to China. That's why we've brought the traffic victims here. That is why we brought the survivors of the political prison camps here so people could hear their stories.

But I think another challenge is how South Korea has responded to this. I think that, for example, the U.S. Congress is united on this. They have passed, two times now, the North Korean Human Rights Act, bipartisan. We have seen the same type of action taking place in Japan. We have seen the United Nations recognize the severity of the human rights abuses in North Korea by appointing a special rapporteur.

But South Korea has yet to pass a North Korean Human Rights Act. There is such a division in South Korea, that is, to me, a huge problem. I am glad that they dispatched diplomats to go to Geneva to bring this issue up with the Human Rights Council, but they should have dispatched diplomats to Beijing.

Representative ROYCE. But you saw that Beijing refused to let Parliamentarian Park into the country. She is not going to be allowed a visa to go into the country.

I passed a resolution here. I have written to 200 parliamentarians, 62 different countries that are part of our International Parliamentarian Coalition on North Korean Refugees and Human Rights. We do have a lot of parliamentarians around the world taking action.

But I would turn it back to this country and I would say, under the prior administration and under this administration we have not pursued policies that would cut off the life support for North Korea. You and I know that over in Treasury, when they put the freeze on assets, Banco of Delta Asia, in order to make it impossible for them to continue their military build-up, that put Kim Jong-il in a terrible position. He could not pay his generals.

We have heard from the defectors, like the former Propaganda Minister, that the resources they get their hands on, the food they get their hands on, goes to feed the military or is sold on the food exchange in Pyongyang for hard currency that they can put into their weapons program.

Fifty percent of the support for that regime comes through illicit activities that we could close down with an anti-proliferation initiative that we once had in place, or by freezing the bank accounts so that they cannot have access to the money to do this.

Why isn't it time to implode this regime or put the kind of pressure that, in the past, worked on bringing down other regimes? South Africa is an example. Sanctions brought down South Africa, or ended apartheid in South Africa. Why not a concerted effort in North Korea?

Instead of the new food aid, which I think, just as in the past, is going to get to the military and help prop them up, why not a serious effort to, once and for all, change this situation since the aid never gets out to the "No-Go" areas in the countryside? We have had French NGOs testify that they followed the food aid being sold on the exchange for hard currency.

Ms. SCHOLTE. Right. Well, you know I totally agree with you. I think it was a real tragedy that George Bush, who cared and actually met with defectors, actually met with the head of Free North Korea Radio, who I quoted in my testimony, actually met with Kang Chul Hwan, a survivor of a political prison camp, actually met with the Hanmee family, one of the families that we helped rescue, had a heart for this issue, but he ended up becoming a money launderer for Kim Jong-il, using our own Treasury Department to return the money from the Bank of Delta Asia scandal.

Representative ROYCE. I will close with this: how can we better deploy Radio Free Asia [RFA] and Voice of America [VOA]? We have heard the defectors now tell us that there are people—including governmental defectors, right? Now we are getting officers and high-ranking civil servants that are listening to VOA and RFA. Are there other ways that we can get information into North Korea, just as we did into the East Bloc, that sort of changed the paradigm? What do you think would be most helpful?

Ms. SCHOLTE. Well, absolutely continuing to support the defectors' broadcasts, like Free North Korea Radio. But also, we do balloon launches regularly. We can tell, by how the regime reacts, the things that are most effective. They absolutely cannot stand the balloon launches. They do not like the defector's radio programs—they have been trying to assassinate Free North Korea Radio director Kim Seong-min for years.

I also think that helping and getting as much information as possible into North Korea through every means possible. We have cell phone technology now. There are a lot of North Koreans that have cell phones. We are trying to get things in through China.

On the food aid, and I tried to articulate this to the Obama administration, Obama is in a unique position because he can articulate—he should be saying, we know you are hungry. We know that most North Koreans spend their days trying to figure out how they are going to feed their families. Obama can send a very strong signal that we want to get food aid, we want to help you, but we are not going to give you the food aid unless we know we can stay there to see it consumed.

The critical thing is being there at the point of consumption. If we are not there at the point of consumption it is 100 percent diverted. We have got to see it utilized by that orphan or by that starving elderly person. We should not provide any food aid unless we can see it at the point of consumption. We can certainly send that message and that is certainly something that President Obama should do.

Representative ROYCE. Thank you. I thank our other very brave witnesses here today.

Chairman SMITH. Let me just ask, if I could, and maybe to you, Ms. Scholte, what has the United Nations, the UNHCR, for example—what is Ban Ki-moon—a Korean, former member of his own government in South Korea who obviously must know, or must be painfully aware of exactly what these refugees go through. What have they done? We know that President Lee [of South Korea] has raised it. He has raised it with the Foreign Minister of China.

I am wondering if there have been any appreciable or discernible changes since that conversation, or no. Why hasn't the UNHCR responded? I would just point out, and you might respond to this, Michael Horowitz, who is one of the architects of the North Korean Human Rights Act of 2004, has underscored and stressed the importance of, if the UNHCR continues to be denied full access to the North Korean refugees, the UN High Commissioner could initiate a binding international arbitration proceeding against the Government of China, as authorized by the UNHCR China Treaty of December 1, 1995. So there is a mechanism. It is ripe, like low-hanging fruit, standing there and waiting to be utilized. What accounts for the apparent lack of interest? Why hasn't it been used?

Ms. SCHOLTE. Well, I am not an expert on that issue, but I know you're going to be talking about it in the next panel.

Chairman SMITH. Yes.

Ms. SCHOLTE. But my understanding is you have to have a country that is willing to pursue that in the United Nations, like to carry the water on the binding arbitration.

Chairman SMITH. Like the United States?

Ms. SCHOLTE. To take the lead on it.

Chairman SMITH. Like the United States?

Ms. SCHOLTE. Like the United States. My understanding is, any country can do that but no one has taken the lead.

As far as UNHCR and Ban Ki-moon, they have been completely ineffectual.

Chairman SMITH. Say that again. Completely what?

Ms. SCHOLTE. Ineffectual. No effect. They have done nothing. They have done neither. I think the UNHCR, though—I will say this, that I know that whenever we have called out to them and appealed to them for help, they have tried to help. The problem is, as long as China refuses to acknowledge that these are refugees and not economic migrants, then the UNHCR's role is minimized because they have to have the permission of the host government to do something. That is why, even though there was funding that was provided in the North Korean Human Rights Act, nothing was ever authorized because you have to have the permission of the host government. So the real problem is China.

Congressman Royce is right, the campaign by the parliamentarians, this is another important thing. They responded. China and North Korea—you can see their reactions, they don't want to make this an international problem. That's why we have to do this, and that's exactly what you're talking about. The international community has to be involved aggressively on this, as well as South Korea and the United States, in taking a lead.

Chairman SMITH. Ms. Jo, you mentioned how the North Korean officials, the security agents, had suggested that the woman was a "bitch" who carried Chinese seed. I am wondering if you detected racial bigotry on the part of North Korean officials toward the Chinese and why the Chinese Government is not upset over that kind of racial bigotry.

Ms. JO. To answer your question, yes, those North Koreans who went to China just to seek food and come back would be less severely treated because they just went to search for food and to lessen the hunger situation.

But those who went to China and became pregnant are deemed by the state as ones who gave up North Korea, who went to China, got pregnant, and are deemed to have wanted to settle down in China and give up North Korea. So that is why they would be seen as a traitor and be even more harshly treated and severely punished.

Chairman SMITH. Do Chinese officials and North Korean agents work together and target refugee communities in China? Yes, Suzanne?

Ms. SCHOLTE. Yes. Absolutely. The North Korean security agents and the Chinese security agents are in total collusion. That is why, for China to deny them refugee status when they full well know that these North Koreans are going to be subjected to horrible abuse when they get sent back—this has been a steady problem. North Korea actually has been using spies that pose as defectors to try to break up these escape routes, the underground railroad.

That is what happened with this latest group. There were North Korean agents that were posing as defectors and that is how this last group got arrested, because the group got sent to detention but some of the defectors got released because they were North Korean agents. So they are definitely working very closely together.

Chairman SMITH. Let me just ask you, in total candor, has the United States raised the issues of these defectors in a robust manner? And that would be the Secretary of State Hilary Clinton, President Obama. We recently had the Vice President of China here in the United States. Was it on the agenda?

Ms. SCHOLTE. I don't know. I was kind of hoping somebody would ask Secretary Clinton that question last week when she testified before the House Foreign Affairs Committee.

Chairman SMITH. We ran out of time.

Ms. SCHOLTE. We did call very strongly on Vice President Biden, President Obama, and Secretary Clinton when the Vice Premier of China was here to raise this issue with China, and we know from friends in the Senate, we know this was raised with them but we don't know whether they raised the issue with the Chinese.

Chairman SMITH. Without revealing any methods—and I'll just ask two more questions—how do family members in China communicate to their family members in North Korea, or do they communicate? If it is going to, in any way, compromise any of those methods, please don't answer it.

Ms. JO. There are basically two methods. Ethnic Chinese-Korean, or "joseonjok" traders or merchants who are able to travel from China to North Korea, would be the ones who would carry cell phones. Through these merchants or traders, they would be in touch with family members in North Korea. Of course, they would be paid, given money to go to carry on these transactions of giving the phones to the family members.

Through that method they would be able to communicate with family members in China, with the family members in North Korea. Another method is, North Korean defectors who resettled in South Korea or the United States would send money or they themselves would actually send the phones to the people, their contacts in China, and that would be another method of being able to communicate with family members in China and North Korea, between the two.

However, now because the North Korea regime knows about the prevalent use of the cell phones, the North Korea regime has brought in cell phone surveillance equipment and is catching these North Korean citizens talking with their relatives back in China. There are known instances of North Korean citizens who have been arrested by the state and incarcerated for the crime of speaking and using a cell phone illegally.

Chairman SMITH. Thank you.

Before going to the second panel, just let me thank you, Ms. Scholte, Ms. Han, Ms. Jo, for your extraordinary testimonies. I would like to ask if there is anything you would like to say before we go to our second panel?

Ms. HAN. Our family of eight was reduced to just three, myself and my two daughters. We are now here. We came to America and we are living in freedom. We are so grateful and thankful for that. While we were in China, the three of us, we were repatriated four times.

That fear, that dread that I felt at that time was that my family, that was reduced to just two daughters, I might even lose my remaining two daughters now. That is the fear and the dread that I felt at that time. I know that the 30 or so North Korean refugees that are being held by China right now, I know that they are feeling the same feeling of dread, fear, and terror. I know that they are looking to the United States to help them and to rescue them.

I just want to conclude by saying that the U.S. Government should forcefully raise this issue and pressure the involved people, the Chinese Government, so that repatriation will not occur and that these refugees will be able to go to South Korea or the United States, and many years down the road that these refugees, these defectors who start new lives in freedom, in free countries, will be able to grow and become successful people, and later on that they in turn will go back to a free North Korea and make that country prosperous just like the other free nations of the world. Thank you.

I would like to conclude by saying that many people throughout the world have signed the petition, as can be seen in this stack of papers here, and many people are fighting for and caring about this issue. So, thank you very much.

Ms. SCHOLTE. I just wanted to thank you very much, Congressman Smith, for your continuing focus on North Korean human rights, and for the media that's here. This is a huge embarrassment to China that more and more people know about this issue, and this is the pivotal time when we can convince the Chinese to change this.

If we do not do it now, there are going to be more and more horror stories as they have told more and more people. It is literally a matter of life and death for those refugees that are being held by China right now. So, I just want to thank you for your continual focus on this.

I did want to mention, on a very positive note, and I just want to share with you that your two witnesses are going to be part of the American delegation for North Korean Freedom Week, which will be in Seoul in April. So for the first time we are going to have North Korean defectors that are part of the American delegation, and I think it is going to send a very positive sign to the people of North Korea.

Ms. Jo. Representative Smith, I would like to conclude by saying that, as Suzanne mentioned previously, the balloon launches, radio broadcasts by stations like Free North Korea Radio, those are important. But the third thing I would like to add is that in Chinese cities, there are many North Korean refugees.

If the U.S. Government, and especially the Korean-American churches in America, can find ways or means to help them to be able to resettle in South Korea or the United States, that would be of great help. In my personal case, Pastor Philip Buck, a Korean-American pastor, was instrumental. He, along with other Korean-American pastors, was instrumental in saving my family and bringing us to the United States. Thank you.

Chairman SMITH. Thank you. Appreciate it so much.

I would like to now ask our second panel to make their way to the witness table, beginning first with T. Kumar.

T. Kumar is Amnesty International's Director for International Advocacy. He has testified before the U.S. Congress on numerous occasions to discuss China's and North Korea's human rights abuses. He has served as a human rights monitor in many Asian countries, as well as in Bosnia, Afghanistan, Guatemala, Sudan, and South Africa.

We will then hear from Mr. Greg Scarlatoiu, who is Executive Director of the Committee for Human Rights in North Korea in Washington, DC. He plans, coordinates, manages, and conducts research and outreach programs to focus world attention on human rights abuses in North Korea. He has authored a weekly radio column broadcast by Radio Free Asia to North Korea for nine years, and numerous English and Korean language articles on Korean peninsula issues.

We will then hear from Mr. Michael Horowitz, who is Senior Fellow at the Hudson Institute in Washington. He is also the Director of the Hudson Institute's Project for Civil Justice Reform, and Project for International Religious Liberty. He has written frequently on North Korean issues and human rights topics and is regularly called to testify and consult with Congress. As I said earlier, he was one of the principle architects of the North Korea Human Rights Act of 2004, and that is putting it mildly in terms of his role. So, thank you, all three, for being here.

We will begin with Mr. Kumar.

STATEMENT OF T. KUMAR, DIRECTOR FOR INTERNATIONAL ADVOCACY, AMNESTY INTERNATIONAL USA

Mr. KUMAR. Thank you very much, Chairman Smith.

First of all, Amnesty International is extremely pleased to be here to express our concern and the information we have about the plight of a group of people in China who have been not only abused by one country, but by two countries—in this case, China and North Korea.

Above all, the people who have fled North Korea have fled out of desperation, out of desperation because of famine, because of political oppression. When they flee, instead of getting protected, they have been abused by the Chinese and also by the North Koreans.

So I would like to, first, give you a glimpse of what is happening in North Korea, for the people of North Korea, for them to be so desperate to flee to a country where they get abused themselves. The famine situation is extremely dire there. Thousands have died.

Even the food distribution system has been staggered into who are supporters of government, then who are not hostile, and hostile to government. So the lowest bottom of the hostile to government category, they do not get enough food. As a result, we have seen famine and death. Also, we have documented numerous abuses in prison camps there, a large number of prison camps there.

So as a result, we have seen thousands crossing over to China to flee this persecution and economic hardship. When they flee, they go through two difficult aspects. The first one is, they are illegals there. Basically, China never accepts them, that they are fleeing because of political persecution or any other reason. So they consider them as economic migrants and their policy is to expel them.

So these people are pretty much illegals, so they survive by the help of some ethnic Koreans in the border areas, working in farms, working in other odd jobs, and some people even beg to survive. Above all, since they are illegals, they get abused by everyone, including the employers, including by the Chinese authorities.

Above all, Chinese authorities have special units that go after these people and track them down to find out who these people are, then deport them. That is one piece of it. The second piece that disturbs everyone is that the Chinese Government also allows North Korean agents to cross into their country and do their arrests and detention and abduct them back to North Korea.

So these people, when they come, they go through hardships on one side and then abuse by North Korean agents, as well as the Chinese agents. China never allows UN groups and also human rights organizations like Amnesty International, or anyone, even to visit or to monitor what is happening to these groups of people.

So these people are kind of left to themselves and fearful anytime of what will happen to them when they get returned. So when they get returned, usually they are considered traitors and people who have betrayed their motherland, in this case, North Korea. So, they have severe punishments.

So imagine before they leave they were normal people, but when they leave out of desperation they become refugees and the Chinese Government never recognizes them as refugees. When they kick them out, they become criminals in their own country.

Now, as you mentioned earlier in your opening remarks, there are new statements coming out from the current new Government of North Korea that anyone who flees will be persecuted more intensely. So when these people return they get detained, tortured, and we have also documented executions. They are sent to labor camps, and we have documented and we have interviewed people who have certified to us that they have seen public executions because of the only crime that they crossed into China just to basically survive.

Coming back to China, the Chinese Government is able to do these things for a couple of reasons. One just relates to North Korea. They have an agreement, a bilateral agreement with North Korea, which is an illegal agreement whereby they agree—both countries have this agreement so that they will return anyone who is here.

The other aspect is the most disturbing fact—the international community's silence on this issue—silence, for different reasons. Above all, the silence of our country, the United States, is also disturbing. You mentioned earlier about the vice president's recent visit. We are not aware of the Obama administration raising this in a vigorous manner. That is extremely disturbing.

So we have some proposals immediately to the Obama administration. There are two dialogues coming up. One is the U.S.-China Security and Economic Dialogue. We want this issue to be one of the other issues—you know, there are other human rights issues in China—to be discussed in a very high-level manner during this Security and Economic Dialogue with China.

Second is, of course, the Annual Human Rights Dialogue. So unless the United States makes this a priority we are going to see that the group of people who have fled and are getting abused by two countries are going to continue being faced with more abuses because of no fault of them. These people are pretty much victims, so we are seeing the victims get victimized through no fault of their own.

The other thing that the United States can do is to raise it in the UN system. I am sure other panelists will be able to discuss that. They should raise it in a more vigorous manner.

Thank you again, Mr. Chairman, for inviting us and we appreciate it. I want our testimony to be on the record.

Chairman SMITH. Mr. Kumar, thank you very much for your testimony.

I would like to now call on our second witness, Mr. Scarlatoiu.

[The prepared statement of Mr. Kumar appears in the appendix.]

STATEMENT OF GREG SCARLATOIU, EXECUTIVE DIRECTOR, COMMITTEE FOR HUMAN RIGHTS IN NORTH KOREA

Mr. SCARLATOIU. Chairman Smith, on behalf of the Committee for Human Rights in North Korea, thank you for inviting me to speak with you at this hearing today.

Our committee considers it essential to draw attention to the case of 30 to 40 North Koreans who have been arrested by China and who now risk being forcibly returned to North Korea, where they most assuredly will be subjected to severe punishment, in violation of international refugee and human rights law.

The fundamental rights to leave a country to seek asylum abroad and not to be forcibly returned to conditions of danger are internationally recognized rights which China and North Korea must be obliged to respect.

Mr. Chair, the Committee for Human Rights in North Korea is a Washington, DC-based non-governmental organization [NGO] established in 2001. Our committee's main statement has been prepared by Chair Roberta Cohen, who is unable to be here today. I will draw upon the statement in my oral remarks.

Over the past two decades, considerable numbers of North Koreans have risked their lives to cross the border into China. They have done so because of starvation, economic deprivation, or political persecution. It is estimated that there are thousands, or tens of thousands, in China today.

Most are vulnerable to forced returns, where they will face persecution and punishment because leaving North Korea without permission is a criminal offense. Yet, to China, all North Koreans are economic migrants and over the years it has forcibly returned tens of thousands to conditions of extreme danger.

We, therefore, submit that North Koreans in China merit international refugee protection for the following reasons:

(1) A definite number of those who cross the border may do so out of a well-founded fear of persecution on political, social, or religious grounds that will accord with the 1951 Refugee Convention.

(2) The reasons why the North Koreans flee to China go beyond the economic realm. Those who cross the border into China for reasons of economic deprivation are often from poorer classes without access to the food and material benefits enjoyed by the privileged political elite.

Subject to Korea's songbun social classification system, their quest for economic survival may be based on political persecution. Examining such cases in a refugee determination process might establish that certain numbers crossing into China for economic survival merit refugee status.

(3) By far the most compelling argument why North Koreans should not be forcibly returned is that most, if not all, fit the category of refugees sur place. As defined by the UN High Commissioner for Refugees [UNHCR], refugees sur place are persons who might not have been refugees when they left their country, but who become refugees at a later date because they have a valid fear of persecution upon return.

North Koreans who leave their country for reasons including economic motives have valid reasons for fearing persecution and punishment upon return. Accordingly, UNHCR has urged China not to forcibly return North Koreans and has proposed a special humanitarian status for them so that they can obtain temporary documentation and access to services and not be repatriated.

China, however, has refused to allow UNHCR access to North Koreans in border areas where it could set up a screening process. It considers itself bound by an agreement it made with North Korea in 1986, obliging both countries to prevent illegal border crossings, which replaced an earlier 1960 agreement.

It also stands by its local law in Jilin Province which requires the return of North Koreans who enter illegally. Both documents stand in violation of China's obligations under the 1951 Refugee Convention, which it signed in 1982, and its membership in

24

UNHCR's Executive Committee and the human rights agreements it has ratified, including the Convention Against Torture and the Convention on the Rights of the Child.

Most North Koreans in China have no rights and are vulnerable to exploitation, forced marriages, and trafficking, as well as to forced returns, where they will face persecution and punishment. Our committee's report, "Lives for Sale: Personal Accounts of Women Fleeing North Korea to China" (2010), documents the experiences of North Korean women in China and the extreme lack of protection for them.

To encourage China to fulfill its international obligations to North Koreans in its territory, our committee puts forward the following recommendations:

(1) The U.S. Congress should consider additional hearings on the plight of North Koreans who cross into China to keep a spotlight on the issue and try to avert forced repatriations to conditions of danger.

(2) Members of Congress should consider supporting the efforts of the Parliamentary Forum for Democracy, established in 2010, so their joint inter-parliamentary efforts can be mobilized in a number of countries on behalf of the North Koreans endangered in China.

(3) The United States should encourage UNHCR to raise its profile on this issue. It further, should lend its full support to UNHCR's appeals and proposals to China and mobilize other governments to do likewise in order to make sure that the provisions of the 1951 Refugee Convention are upheld and the work of this important UN agency enhanced.

(4) Together with other concerned governments, the United States should give priority to raising the forced repatriation of North Koreans with Chinese officials, but in the absence of a response should bring the issue before international refugee and human rights fora.

(5) The United States should consider promoting a multi-lateral approach to the problem of North Koreans leaving the country.

(6) The United States should consider ways to enhance its readiness to increase the number of North Korean refugees and asylum seekers admitted to this country. Other countries should be encouraged as well to take in more North Korean refugees and asylum seekers until such time as they no longer face persecution and punishment in their country.

Thank you, Mr. Chairman and members of the Commission. I look forward to answering any questions you might have.

Chairman SMITH. Mr. Scarlatoiu, thank you very much for your testimony and for your insights, as well as your very specific recommendations, and Mr. Kumar's as well. That was an extraordinary testimony.

Now I would like to welcome Mr. Horowitz and ask him to present this testimony.

STATEMENT OF MICHAEL HOROWITZ, SENIOR FELLOW, HUDSON INSTITUTE

Mr. HOROWITZ. Thank you, Mr. Chairman.

At this hearing there's been much focus, and rightly so, on the conduct and evils committed by the Government of China and by the Government of North Korea. What I hope to provide and what I think is very much called for is further thought on how to make those protests, how to make those complaints, more effective in ways that reach China.

My own experience with China, and I think you will confirm it, Mr. Chairman, is that it is in many ways the least ideological country in the world. It is all an issue of cost and gain. There are ways of imposing costs on China for its conduct toward these refugees that I think need exploration.

Let me set out some that I think will be the most effective. The first is really to thank you, Mr. Smith and colleagues like Congressman Wolf, Congressman Royce, who live and die these human rights issues. I wish there were more of you in Congress. This is an occasion to lament the death of Tom Lantos. I think, had he been alive, Congress would have spoken on a bipartisan basis and much more clearly. And former colleagues like Tony Hall are as well deeply missed in not having made this a much more bipartisan issue than it ought to be.

I do hope in that regard that we can reach Minority Leader Nancy Pelosi, because when she was a mere Member of Congress her voice was one of the loudest, and clearest, and bravest on human rights violations by the Chinese Government.

If somehow Minority Leader and former Speaker Pelosi can regain that voice, I think China will sit up and listen because there really will be a bipartisan coalition. So, reaching Nancy Pelosi seems to me one way of rescuing these 33 people and changing China's policies.

In the Senate, we need to make up for the loss of Sam Brownback and Evan Bayh, who spoke so clearly and on a bipartisan basis. And I am hoping that Senator Brown, that Senator Rubio, that others join and that we have this kind of bipartisan strength that China will recognize and respond to.

The second, and it has been mentioned, is the Korean-American community. I have spent the last five years trying to engage that community, as the Jewish community was engaged on the campaign for Soviet Jewry, as the African-American community was engaged on the campaign against the apartheid regime.

I am absolutely convinced that in this Nation of immigrants, which always hears the cries of Americans who speak of the torture of their brothers and sisters in their home countries, that the Korean-American community, unbeknownst to itself, has the power to change China's mind and shift American policy and create a paradigm shift on China's part and in the treatment of these refugees.

Let me put it this way: Neither the Democratic nor the Republican Party would be willing for a second, no matter what China's pressures would be, to risk the loss of the votes in support of the Korean-American community over the next 25 or 30 years. The leadership of the Korean-American community must make this its signature issue: The murder of their brothers and sisters. And we have ways of reaching that community, as Scoop Jackson reached a reluctant Jewish community.

So there's another leadership role for this Commission and for you, again, Mr. Chairman. I would have Members of Congress call in the leaders, the church leaders in the Korean-American community, as Scoop Jackson called in the leaders of the Jewish community, and tell them to have a prayer Sunday for North Korea at 3,000 Korean-American churches with voter registration booths outside the churches.

That will change things dramatically within the administration and China will see that it cannot use the business community, it cannot leverage the political community because America will listen to an aroused, engaged Korean-American community, which has not yet happened.

Third, of course, the administration. And it's been mentioned, food aid should be distributed on a needs basis. This new deal that was made has got to be made with careful attention to the fair distribution of the food on a needs basis.

But the core of it all, and it's a problem of both this administration and the prior one, is the lack of a Helsinki Strategy approach to dealing with China and North Korea issues.

A Helsinki Strategy would, as Suzanne and others have said, put human rights issues right in the basket of things that are negotiated as we talk of all weapons issues with North Korea. It has been relegated to a so-called second track. The Chinese get it: It doesn't matter.

Whenever an American official speaks, as the Vice President did during the Xi visit, the Chinese understand that that's for domestic political consumption and it doesn't really reflect the policy of the United States to prioritize issues of human rights. Let me say, Ronald Reagan understood all this.

You know why, Mr. Chairman? Because he had been president of a union. I think if we had the AFL–CIO replacing the State Department in these negotiations there would be this understanding: That raising human rights issues is important not only for moral reasons, but it would make us far more powerful on the weapons issues, where we offer and sell the same product and get the same promises and give money and get no response, as will be the case this time.

And any union negotiator would understand that if the only thing on our table is the weapons issue, we are signaling to China and to North Korea, "You've got something we want, how much do we have to pay you for it?" All the leverage goes on the other side. Anybody from the Teamster's union would get it in a second, Mr. Chairman; and that's what we need, the kind of shrewdness in bargaining that I find lacking here and the power of a Helsinki Strategy.

From that follows—and I want to get specific about the 33—Bob King is a very decent, caring man, who is our Special Envoy for North Korean Human Rights, but as I have said, he's on the second track. It's so low as not to count, really. And the Chinese take Bob King's assignment as the negotiator for the 33, I fear, as a signal that they can deport those 33 and nothing will happen to U.S.-China relations. We need to get—and I hope this Commission will ensure this—the Secretary to become engaged in the negotiation over the lives of those 33 and the others. That's the signal that this administration has not sent but needs to send.

And I think Michael Posner, a friend and a good man, needs to throw around his weight a little bit more and pound his shoe on the table because he's been ignored, as Frank Wolf pointed out at the last hearing, over the Xi visit. And I think Michael needs to seriously indicate to his colleagues in the State Department that he's ready to resign if those 33 are deported. I think he has a moral obligation to resign, frankly, if any of those 33 are sent to death camps and if this administration sends the kind of low-interest, low-priority signal it has sent.

And finally, Mr. Chairman, the United Nations. There is the key leverage point. I have set it out in a memo that I distributed that I hope will be part of the record, and it was also set out in a remarkable letter sent by Senator Brownback and Congressman Wolf to former UN Secretary General Kofi Annan: All refugees, as everybody has said, are migrants because they are persecuted on their return. You don't need to know anything else. The United Nations has the right to access those refugees the second they cross the Tumen River, and the obligation to insist upon it. But as you pointed out, Mr. Chairman, there is Article 14 of the China-UNHCR treaty, which is a powerful tool that I call on this Commission, and everybody who cares, to begin exploiting. That's true of the South Koreans who are protesting against China. They ought to be protesting to Ban Ki-moon, himself a Korean, because the United Nations has the ability to change the whole ball game.

Let me just state, Section 14 of the treaty says that, "Any dispute between the Government of China and the UNHCR, arising out of or relating to this agreement, dealing with refugees, shall be settled amicably or by negotiation or other mode of settlement. But if this fails, such a dispute shall be submitted to arbitration at the request of either party."

And Suzanne Scholte, for whom I have the most profound respect, said that some other country needs to negotiate it. That's not even accurate in that regard. The UNHCR can do it. Here's the last sentence: "If, within 30 days of the request for arbitration, neither party has appointed an arbitrator"—and we're talking about China here—"Either party may request the president of the International Court of Justice to appoint an arbitrator. The arbitral award shall contain a statement of the reasons on which it is based and shall be accepted by the parties as the final adjudication of this dispute." Imagine the price China would have to pay if they were getting sued by the United Nations.

And let me say, Mr. Chairman, in conclusion, that the North Korea Human Rights Act is explicit. It said that the failure of the United Nations to bring that arbitration proceeding provided under Article 14 of the treaty was, and I quote, "An abdication by the UNHCR of one its core responsibilities."

Now, Mr. Chairman, we finance the United Nations and the UNHCR. China doesn't put any money in, we do. It's time we got our money's worth. It's time we really protected the lives of those 33 and the others, and we have the means to do it. And I am hopeful that this Commission, and frankly, members of the Appropriations Committee who provide that support for the United Nations and for the UNHCR, will call in the High Commissioner, will call in Ban Ki-moon, will call their colleagues in the South Korean National Assembly, and begin putting the heat on the United Nations to stop being passive and, frankly, stop appeasing China and begin enforcing their treaty obligations and responsibilities.

Thank you, Mr. Chairman, for permitting me to testify.

Chairman SMITH. Thank you very much, Mr. Horowitz, for your testimony, and very valid—and I think very effective—recommendations as to what all of us should be doing, including this Commission.

I just want to thank all three of you for reminding us that whatever the intent was originally for leaving North Korea—as Ms. Han pointed out, her husband went across the Tumen River to bring back a sack of rice because their family, his family, was starving—for that he was imprisoned and killed, and then they became marked persons themselves. It is what you are going to be forcibly repatriated to that dictates whether or not you're a refugee, and I think for some to miss that very obvious point needs to be underscored.

All three of you pointed that out, that whatever the original intent, if they go back they're marked people. They have a huge target on their backs and they either go to execution or to hideous torture that awaits them. So, thank you for reminding us of that, all three of you.

Let me just ask, again, you heard Michael Horowitz talk about the importance of focusing on the United Nations, and all three of you did make mention of that as well, and the UNHCR. But invoking this mechanism that he spoke of, do you find that, Mr. Kumar and Mr. Scarlatoiu, to be something that needs to be pursued as well? Do you find that a very effective mechanism? Mr. Kumar?

Mr. KUMAR. I am not aware of this. I mean, not in depth, like Mike is aware. But that mechanism, as he explained, should be exploited. The United States can play a role, by the way. The UNHCR has to be pressured by the U.S. administration. I am sure there are representatives who are there in the UN High Commission, and they have a mechanism in their body to exploit this. I have never heard of it.

I even asked Mike before the hearing, is there any precedent for this when we discussed this. Otherwise, this will become a precedent. That would be a great thing, by the way. So I will recommend that the U.S. administration—we should urge the United Nations, but you know how the United Nations operates.

They need member countries to exert pressure—the United States, along with other countries, South Korea as well—and put some pressure on the UNHCR to exploit this mechanism to see whether that's something achievable. If that can be achieved, that would be a ground-breaking avenue to protect North Korean refugees, as well as other refugees who may be in the same plight.

Mr. SCARLATOIU. Chairman Smith, in the fourth recommendation that I respectfully brought to your attention today we suggest that we should give priority to raising the forced repatriation of North Koreans with Chinese officials, but also absent a response we should bring the issue before international refugee and human rights fora.

Certainly UNHCR's Executive Committee, the UN Human Rights Council, as well as the General Assembly of the United Nations, should all be expected to call on China by name to carry out its obligations under refugee and human rights law and enact legislation to codify these obligations so that North Koreans will not be expelled if their lives or freedom are in danger.

I have also mentioned the need for a multi-lateral approach to the issue of North Koreans leaving the country. Their exodus affects more than just China, it concerns South Korea—the Republic of Korea, most notably, whose constitution offers citizenship to North Koreans; countries in east and southeast Asia, eastern and western Europe, as well as Mongolia and the United States, are also affected.

A multi-lateral approach should be designed, an approach that finds solutions for North Koreans based on principles of non-refoulement and human rights and humanitarian protection.

Chairman SMITH. Thank you.

Mr. Horowitz?

Mr. HOROWITZ. I have spoken with the High Commissioner for Refugees. It just boggles my mind, Mr. Chairman. He talks about the pressure from the Chinese. He doesn't talk about pressure from the United States, which pays his electric bills. It is time now to put the heat on the United Nations and, frankly, with the Secretary General himself being Korean and a former Foreign Minister of Korea, we've got the leverage to apply.

Our complaining, even if the State Department were as committed as I hope they would be, won't move China as much as the notion that they were isolated and the United Nations and the UNHCR were suing them for what everybody acknowledges, including the United Nations, is a clear violation of all of the applicable treaties. So I think the time has come to put the heat on and put the focus on the United Nations, and that would be true even if there wasn't an arbitration proceeding in the China UNHCR treaty.

Chairman SMITH. To the best of your knowledge have the picketers and the protesters who rightfully have focused on North Korea and certainly on China, but to the best of my knowledge they have not focused on the leverage that the United States could bring, and I don't think they have sufficiently focused on the leverage they could bring to bear on the United Nations itself.

Mr. HOROWITZ. Exactly. I think that we need to focus on the United States. As I've said, we need to focus on moving the negotiations from the level—good as he is—of Bob King to the level of the Secretary. I think we need to make Michael Posner understand that his tenure and the respect he earns will be contingent on the United States elevating, by orders of magnitude, the priority of this negotiation.

But I think most of all we need to put the onus on the United Nations, whose treaties are being violated and whose response has been literally non-existent. That must change and the United States has the leverage to make it happen, I believe.

Chairman SMITH. You know, we've called this hearing as an emergency hearing precisely because, for those individuals affected—maybe it's 33, it might be a few more, nobody knows for sure—their lives are in imminent danger of persecution or execution. It seems to me that with the focus—and I do thank the media for being here, for amplifying the concern and the message of all of our very distinguished witnesses.

But from hearing from Ms. Jo and Ms. Han earlier, we heard from people who lived, are survivors, and shame on us, frankly, in the Congress, shame on us in the United States and at the United Nations, and every other body that cares about human rights and the rule of law if we don't make this the case. This is the case. I think the three of you have very eloquently underscored why this is the time to act. I deeply appreciate your testimonies because they couldn't come in a more timely fashion.

So I would like to just ask you if there's anything else either of you would like to add to the record before we conclude this hearing.

Also, Roberta Cohen, who you, Mr. Scarlatoiu, spoke somewhat from her testimony, that her full statement be also made a part of the record.

So if there's anything you'd like to add, to our distinguished witnesses. Yes, Greg?

[The written statement of Ms. Cohen appears in the appendix.]

Mr. SCARLATOIU. Congressman Smith, thank you very much for continuing to pay attention to this very important set of issues. Our two main challenges as North Korean human rights experts and advocates are that North Korean issues are extraordinarily important, but they always compete with other extraordinarily important issues.

Even when we pay attention to North Korea's military provocations, missile launches, sinking of South Korean ships, it is very difficult to keep North Korean human rights at the top of the agenda. So, once again, thank you so much for your efforts.

Additionally, I would like to conclude by reminding everyone, this point has been made here today, that we the people of the United States of America pay for one-third of UNHCR's budget, and thus we should have tremendous leverage when it comes to this issue of the North Korean refugees in China.

Chairman SMITH. Excellent point.

Mr. SCARLATOIU. Thank you, sir.

Chairman SMITH. Mr. Kumar?

Mr. KUMAR. Thank you, Chairman. I would recommend focusing on what Mike mentioned about the specific UN mechanism in place, which, as I understand, there is no precedent. So, it is better to explore that. I wonder whether the Commission, or any other committee, can explore it as a study to see whether there is something there. Then if that's agreeable, then it can start moving in that direction. Thank you.

Chairman SMITH. Mr. Horowitz?

Mr. HOROWITZ. Mr. Chairman, I am about to flatter you, and I think you know me well enough to know that I am not doing it for any other reason but that I so deeply believe it. But I will say that in Japan there is this tradition of declaring living human beings as national treasures. I put you in that category for your persistence on human rights issues and I cannot thank you enough.

I want to say just one other thing. Again, I want to get back to the Reagan point. When Ronald Reagan dealt with the former Soviet Union, there are these stories of how the Russian Ambassador came to the American Secretary of State and said, "You know, I want to talk to the President about missiles and all these real issues. Every time I come into his office, all he wants to talk about are Pentecostals and Jewish refuseniks. Is he really serious? What's going on here?"

Secretary Schultz said, "Listen, I've got the same problem. That's what he talks about. If you want to deal with the United States you're going to have to come to term on these human rights issues." Reagan cared. But as I said, he was also a union negotiator and he understood that that was the means of putting the other side on the defensive. He didn't brag about success, but it's that sense of priority.

So I want it understood, Mr. Chairman, that your passion for human rights is not "merely" because you care about vulnerable human beings; it is a shrewd, strategic means of getting better deals on the weapons side. Because once we start raising those issues, they'll do anything to keep the issues off the table. That's where they're vulnerable.

If we can have, not just voices in the wilderness, but this being the real priority interest of the United States in terms of policies, as Ronald Reagan dealt with the Soviet Union or Scoop Jackson understood, I think we will get better deals on weapons. I think we will begin to have a means of peacefully imploding the regime in North Korea, of sending a signal to China that keeping this regime in business costs them more than it gets them.

And I will say one last thing about China. Every leader there lived through the Cultural Revolution. In personal terms, they understand the evils of North Korea better than anybody else does because they lived through it. Only, what they understand further is that this has gone on for 65 years, not for a couple of years.

The only problem is we haven't made them pay a price for that. Once we begin escalating that price, as Reagan understood in dealing with the Soviet Union, I think they will find it counterproductive in terms of their national interests to continue supporting this regime. So, keep it up, Mr. Chairman, and we will have peaceful change in North Korea. Thank you.

Mr. KUMAR. Congressman, I have just one last thing.

Chairman SMITH. Yes, Mr. Kumar?

Mr. KUMAR. Is it possible for the Commission to urge the U.S. Ambassador to China, Ambassador Locke, to visit this body and submit a report about the plight of North Korean refugees? That will add pressure on China and also get an official line from the U.S. administration on what they think and what should be done. Thank you.

Chairman SMITH. A very good point, Mr. Kumar. We will explore that and ask him if he will do that. All of you have made extraordinary contributions to what we ought to be doing, next steps, as well as an understanding of where we are now. I would agree with you fully, Mr. Horowitz. I broke my eye teeth on human rights on the Soviet Jewry issue. My first trip was to Moscow and Leningrad in 1982, the second year of my first term, and I learned very quickly every since then that when human rights are subordinated, put on the back bench, that all the other issues, whether it be intellectual property rights or trade agreements of any kind, and especially arms control, they all are weaker, or they are ineffective in terms of implementation.

Get the human rights piece right and all the others follow, not the other way around. Unfortunately, the genius of the North Korean Human Rights Act was to mainstay and mainstream the human rights issues in North Korea, as we ought to be doing everywhere else, and its implementation has been far less, both under Bush as well as under Obama. That needs to be corrected. All of you have made very eloquent statements and we will act upon them.

This hearing is adjourned.

[Whereupon, at 4:27 p.m. the hearing was adjourned.]

APPENDIX

PREPARED STATEMENTS

—————

PREPARED STATEMENT OF SUZANNE SCHOLTE

MARCH 5, 2012

Senator Sherrod Brown and Congressman Chris Smith and Members of the Commission, thank you for so quickly responding to the urgent crisis facing North Korean refugees recently arrested in China.

Congressman Smith, you will remember that in September you hosted a hearing with a North Korean defector, Kim Hye Sook, the longest serving survivor of the North Korean political prison camps. She spent twenty eight years in a political prison camp. I mention her today because the reason she was jailed at the age of 13 with her entire family in Bukchang political prison camp, where her brother and sister are still imprisoned, was simply because her grandfather allegedly had escaped to South Korea. She is a living example of how the regime retaliates against three generations of a family if just one family member flees North Korea.

As draconian as these measures have been, the current situation is even more critical for the North Korean defectors recently arrested in China, most face execution because of three factors. First, the Kim Jung Un regime announced in December that the entire family and relatives should be annihilated if any family member fled during the 100 day mourning period following Kim Jong Il's death.

Second, among the group of over thirty that were arrested in February are defectors who have family members who have successfully defected to South Korea. In fact, the parents of a 19 year old girl arrested in China have pleaded that their daughter be allowed to commit suicide rather than be repatriated to North Korea. There is also a 71 year old mother, who has a daughter in South Korea, and a mother and her 20 day old baby, as well as a 16 year old boy whose brother is in South Korea. In many cases, these refugees are trying desperately to be reunited with each other as they are the only survivors of families destroyed by starvation and persecution.

Third, China is providing information to North Korea about the intentions of the refugees it has arrested informing the North Korean security agents if these refugees were trying to flee to South Korea. Because of this collusion, the Chinese government is complicit in pre-meditated murder because it knows that those refugees, when repatriated to North Korea, face execution.

By refusing to honor its international treaty commitments and colluding with North Korea to repatriate these refugees, China has created a violent and lawless situation where eighty percent of North Korean females are subjected to human trafficking and North Korean agents are allowed to freely roam around China assassinating humanitarian workers and hunting down refugees.

Imagine this for a moment: the Chinese government, which wants to be seen as a responsible international leader, refuses to allow the United Nations High Commissioner for Refugees, whose sole purpose is to help nations address refugee problems, access to these refugees but has no problem allowing North Korean spies and assassins free reign.

This collusion between North Korea and China proves most definitely that China cannot hide behind its claim that these refugees are economic migrants, and not subjected to the international treaties China has signed.

China knows full well—and has known for decades—that when they force these North Koreans back to North Korea they face certain torture, certain imprisonment and increasingly execution for fleeing their homeland.

According to Kim Seong Min of Free North Korea Radio, which has informants in both North Korea's and China's security operations, China began separating North Korean defectors into two groups based on whether they were trying to escape to South Korea starting in at least 2008. We suspect this was part of the crack down before the Beijing Olympics and the enormous fear China had about the world coming to know about their cruel treatment of North Korean refugees.

Ju Seong-ha, a reporter for Donga-Ilbo and Kim Yong-hwa, the Representative of North Korean Defectors' Protection Association, both defectors themselves, have described how China uses a different color stamp on the interrogation papers for those defectors who were attempting to get to South Korea.

China is literally marking these refugees for death before they are repatriated.

We are at a critical point in this fight for the lives of the North Korean refugees and urgent action and attention is needed. If we do not convince China to reverse its repatriation policy and work with the international community on this issue, the refugees in China's custody face death.

In closing, I want to cite a number of arguments that should be used to convince China that it is in their best interest to follow their international treaty obligations and work with the international community. In fact, China is not only causing this refugee crisis, but prolonging it.

First, China fears an increasing flow of refugees if it allows refugees safe passage to South Korea, but China's actions are ensuring that there will always be refugees by relieving Kim Jong Un of taking any measures that would improve conditions in North Korea. The fact is that North Koreans are fleeing North Korea out of desperation. They know the considerable risk they are taking to flee to China but they keep risking their lives to pursue this action out of desperation. Furthermore, most North Koreans who have resettled in South Korea and other nations want to go back to North Korea once conditions improve in their homeland. China has desired that the Kim regime adopt China-style reforms but by forcefully sending fleeing North Koreans back to North Korea, China relieves any pressure for Kim to improve conditions in North Korea so the citizens do not want to flee.

Second, China's future will be much brighter for its people if its government works with South Korea rather than kowtows to the dictator in North Korea. The two countries celebrate the twentieth anniversary of their diplomatic ties this year and enjoy a robust trade relationship. South Korean culture is very popular in China, and many Chinese tourists travel to South Korea. Working with South Korea on this issue will have a positive benefit to their future relationship because it is inevitable that Korea one day will be reunified. With the increasing amount of information flowing into North Korea and more and more North Koreans becoming aware of the truth, brutal dictatorship of Kim Jong-Un is doomed to end.

Third, all the remedies for resolving this issue are immediately at hand to ensure no burden on China including a UN sanctioned agency with an office in Beijing, the UNHCR; a humanitarian network and a strong commitment from South Korea and the United States to help resettle refugees.

Finally, China needs to be reminded of what this regime really thinks of the Chinese people. Kim Jong il had a long established policy known as "Block the yellow wind"—as he was resistant to adopting any China style reforms. His racist contempt for the Chinese people was evident in his ordering of his border guards to beat the bellies of pregnant North Korean females who had been repatriated because their unborn babies were half Chinese.

Now, that more and more people around the world are becoming aware of the North Korean refugee crisis and calling upon China not to force these refugees back to North Korea, this is a perfect opportunity for China to show great leadership and work with the international community, rather than kowtowing to a brutal dictatorship, frequently cited as one of the world's worst regimes.

I want to close by recognizing one of your colleagues, Assemblywoman Park Sun Young of the Korean National Assembly, who began a hunger strike on February 21 across the street from the Chinese Embassy in Seoul calling for China not to repatriate these refugees and vowing to continue her vigil until death unless the North Korean refugees are allowed safe passage to Seoul. This brave woman collapsed on Friday and was rushed to the hospital. She understands the consequences for these refugees, and we hope that parliamentarians as well as governments around the world will join her in calling upon China to end their brutal repatriation policy and stop sending North Koreans to their death.

SUBMITTED WITH THIS TESTIMONY

(1) Letter to Hu Jintao by North Korean defector and reporter Seongha Ju, The Donga Daily

(2) "Kkot Dong San" A Hill Filled with Flowers, an essay about the reeducation camp where tens of thousands were sent and died following repatriation from China

(3) Red stamps for those escaping to South Korea for freedom? The behind-the-scene deal between China and North Korea

* * *

LETTER TO HU JINTAO BY NORTH KOREAN DEFECTOR AND REPORTER SEONGHA JU,
THE DONGA DAILY

[TRANSLATION OF LETTER PUBLISHED IN DONGA ILBO ON FEBRUARY 14, 2012]

Dear President Hu Jintao,

The heartrending cry of the family of North Korean refugees arrested in China last week, encouraged me to write to you through this newspaper. Now you are the only person that can save their life.

I am also a refugee from North Korea that fled via China to South Korea through severe hardships. Feeling, with every fiber of my body and soul, the fear and agony of the refugees facing impending repatriation to North Korea, I am desperately writing this letter word by word, hoping this will be the last lifeline to which the arrested can resort.

China has, to date, repatriated arrested North Korean refugees to Pyongyang, and will also do the same this time.

Mr. President, however, please be noted that Pyongyang's punishment of the refugees has grown unprecedently and incomparably severe. Of recent, Pyongyang deems defection as the most serious menace to their regime, taking the most hawkish approach including on-the-spot execution of the refugees on the border.

The punishment has got even harsher since Kim Jong-Il's death, and Pyongyang reportedly even issued an instruction to annihilate the entire family and relatives of the refugees that defected during 100 days' mourning period. Under such atmosphere, it is as clear as daylight that the refugees will be subject to an exemplary execution or imprisonment in the concentration camp for political prisoners, immediately after being taken to North Korea.

China has been strengthening coordination with North Korea to prevent defection in various areas including putting barbed-wire fence on the border, tracking down refugees, patrolling the border, detecting the radio wave, etc.

China's concern about Pyongyang regime's stability, is not incomprehensible. No matter how it may be, however, by when will you assume the villain role to drive refugees to death? By when will you support the regime that cannot control its people without public execution and deadly concentration camps?

Throughout the last decade, tens of thousands of refugees were taken back from China to North Korea, many among whom have passed away from harsh punishment and famine. China also stands liable to their death. When will you realize the fact that China is losing North Koreans' public trust whenever you fell the refugees off the cliff of the death one by one?

Many of the arrested have their family in South Korea. Most of them are sons, daughters, parents and siblings of South Koreans. Among them is a teenager who has a brother and a sister in South but no other family in North. The brother and the sister are shivering like wounded deer in the corner of a room, off all food and drink, at the news that their younger brother, who they were to bring to South with the money they scraped up with hard shores at the cafeteria.

Parents of an arrested girl, crying bitterly in front of the South Korea's Ministry of Foreign Affairs and Trade, pleaded to send poison to their daughter if her rescue is impossible. They want her to commit suicide in China rather than to be killed by cruel punishment in North Korea. Other family's feeling is just alike.

Their repatriation to Pyongyang will leave dozens of their family in South Korea in lifelong agony, nightmare and sense of guilt. There are tens of thousands of separated families in two Koreas already living like that. How can I describe their pain in mere writing?

Mr. President, this year we have the 20th anniversary of the establishment of diplomatic relations between China and South Korea. Every Korean and the whole world are keeping keen eyes on you. Please allow them to meet their family again with joy. I desperately ask your generosity. Please let us all applaud you with deep appreciation.

Sincerely Yours,
Seongha Ju, Reporter of The Donga Daily

* * *

"Kkot Dong San" A Hill Filled with Flowers, an essay about the reeducation camp where tens of thousands were sent and died following repatriation from China

[http://blog.donga.com/nambukstory/archives/23738]

Sung Ha Joo 2/14/2012 8:00AM

There is a certain "Kkot-Dong-San."

It is a hill by a reeducation camp in Jungsan-kun, Pyong-Nam in North Korea. The reeducation camp is an imitation of the Soviet Union's forced labor camps in the past. Those who are sentenced to several years due to attempts at escaping must farm under the influence of hunger and ruthless whipping that one can hardly imagine.

If the people in these camps die from hunger or beating, they are buried in the Kkot-Dong-San. Tens of thousands of corpses are buried there. Several corpses are buried in a single hole, and when it's full, other corpses were buried over these graves. In the winter when the earth is frozen, the burial process becomes merely a covering process. The corpses are wrapped in a plastic wrap, and a penicillin bottle with the name and birthday is hung around each corpse's neck.

The human skull protruding from the ground as well as pieces of cloth and vinyl paper flapping with wind reminds one looking from afar of a flower field, which is why the reeducation camp prisoners call the hill "Kkot-Dong-San." It also reflects the prisoners' desperate wish to get away from hell at least in their deathbed.

Though often political prisoner camps are considered the epitome of North Korea's human rights violations, the reeducation camps are actually worse. Political prisoners are slaves for life. Slaves are assets. If they only work under the influence of whipping, they become very good workers. Products made from political prisoner camps are considered to have the best quality of all products in North Korea.

On the other hand, when they are released from the prisoner camps and enter reeducation camps, they are merely "human trash" to the North Korean elites. They would prefer seeing these prisoners die from persecution.

A woman who was arrested and taken to Jungsan reeducation camp in 2000 said that among 2000 people with whom she first entered the camp, only 200 people were still living after 7 months. It is the same with other reeducation camps. North Korean defectors who were in charge of disposing corpses in 1998 for six months said that they disposed of 859 corpses in total.

The majority will die due to malnutrition. In a reeducation camp, other living things such as rats and insects are on the verge of extinction because the prisoners put whatever they see alive into their mouths.

In reeducation camps, the day that one will finally die is estimated by a fist. If a fist can go in between your crack vertically, you are on your way to dying, if a fist can go in horizontally, you are dying, and if a fist can go in in both ways, you will not survive.

Just like that, I know so well what it is to be dying. I had also failed escaping and been classified as a political prisoner. As a result, I frequented the security department's torture chambers, prisons, and labor camps. Only when I was on the verge of death, weighing only 90 lbs, was I released.

After I came to South Korea, I have been writing about North Korea for 10 years. Many times I cried because I had experienced the same pain that other North Koreans are experiencing. To me, North Korea is pain and tears. I cannot step away from my keyboard if I think about my fellow North Koreans who are suffering and dying.

I received a list of North Korean refugees recently arrested in China. O, how painful. . .

Kim Jung Un declared that anyone defecting after Kim Jung Il died will have his or her family killed down to three generations. China does not feel guilty at all even after pushing the North Korean refugees close to death. The picture of "Kkot-Dong-San" where crows linger above the sad faces of those being sent back to North Korea is vivid in my mind.

I plead to you not just as a reporter, but also as a person who has experienced what a Hell is. If you happen to see an idol worship or group gymnastics performance and waves of other flowers in Pyongyang, please remember the labor reeducation camp "Kkotdongsan." Please don't forget the nameless dead who are being wrapped and buried in "Kkoddongsan."

Even if it's only once in a while. . . Please . . ..

* * *

RED STAMPS FOR THOSE ESCAPING TO SOUTH KOREA FOR FREEDOM? THE BEHIND-
THE-SCENE DEAL BETWEEN CHINA AND NORTH KOREA

[http://blog.donga.com/nambukstory/archives/24333]

2012/02/22 8:00 am Sungha Joo

It is discovered that in the process of deporting the North Korean refugees back
to North Korea, the Chinese government has been informing to the North Korean
government whether the captured refugees had escaped North Korea to head to
South Korea or not.

There is a high possibility that the North Korean refugees who intended to escape
to South Korea will either be detained in a political prisoners camp or be executed
after they are deported. It was the North Korean government that told the Chinese
government to determine the refugees' intended destinations.

The Tumen Public Security Bureau in China announced on the 21st that the Chinese Public Security Bureau has been receiving natural resources such as logs and
minerals from North Korea in return for deportation of the refugees back to North
Korea.

They (Tumen Public Security Bureau) said that "Recently China has been informing North Korea about the refugees intending to head to South Korea by using different colors of stamp on the files".

China has been using different colors of stamp that they agreed upon with North
Korea each month, for example red in January and blue in February, instead of
writing down "to South Korea", in order to avoid leaving obvious evidence that they
have been assisting North Korea.

It is reported that due to the enlarging issue about refugees beyond the nation,
China came up with this idea of using different colors of stamp to inform North
Korea if the refugees were heading to South Korea.

When China had a good relationship with North Korea, they even handed over
all the interrogation files to North Korea and moreover, during the late 1990's, it
is witnessed that a North Korean investigator, disguised as a Chinese investigator,
came over to China and interrogated the refugees.

The former North Korean lieutenant and the director of a North Korean broad-
casting station, Sungmin Kim, said on the 21st that when he was being interrogated, "I was criticizing the political system of North Korea to a Chinese investigator who seemed to be compassionate and understanding, but later when I was
being deported back to North Korea, the same man welcomed me back not as a Chinese investigator but as a North Korean personnel agent".

If China does not inform North Korea about the refugees' intent to escape to
South Korea, the refugees will have a better chance in living even after they get
deported. Since it is difficult for the North Korean refugee investigators to go over
to China to investigate, the refugees only need to deny that they were intending on
fleeing to South Korea and endure the tortures but could still spare their lives.

However, it is relatively easy to find out about the destinations of the refugees
in China because the refugees hoping to head to South Korea are taken under custody along with the people who help them to their freedom.

It is reported that the Chinese government has been assisting in capturing the
refugees and handpicked those who are to be executed and in return, they received
logs and minerals from North Korea.

The bitter refugees witnessed that the compensations for the refugees change
from time to time, but usually they consist of logs from Mt. Baekdu and iron ore
from Musan mine. The exchange of the refugees and the natural resources started
since 1998 and has continued until now like a tradition.

China sends back arrested North Korean refugees mainly through Tumen (located
on the opposite side of Du-Man River in On-Sung, North Hamkyung Province) and
Dandong (located on the opposite side of Ap-Nok River in Shin-ee, North Pyong-An
Province). They also use any other bridges that connect China and North Korea.

Even at just Tumen, more than 3,000 refugees have been deported back to North
Korea within a year. From this, it is estimated that more than 5,000 refugees are
deported back to North Korea every year.

The Chinese government detains the refugees at the Tumen prisoner camp and
when the camp fills up, they transport the refugees back to North Korea once or
twice a week by buses. In the past, they used military trucks for the transportation,
but since a lot of the refugees took their own lives by throwing themselves out the
truck into the river at the bordering bridges, they changed trucks to buses.

Typically, refugees who are captured around Tumen like Yanji are deported back
within two weeks, but if the refugees are captured somewhere farther away, the in-

vestigation takes longer. Tumen prisoner camp is meant for foreign criminals, but there are only refugees there now.

In this camp, North Korean refugees are repeatedly beaten and sexually harassed while they are stricken with fear before repatriation. North Korean refugees who have already experienced this prisoner camp said that at times, on the pretense of delaying repatriation, the camp officials rape the prisoners.

————

PREPARED STATEMENT OF SONGHWA HAN

MARCH 5, 2012

Hello, my name is Song Hwa Han and I came to the United States with my two daughters in 2008 as refugees, following the passage of the North Korean Human Rights Act in the United States Congress in 2004. The lowest class of people in North Korea have a most desperate and earnest plea. That plea is to be freed and liberated to freedom of human rights from the worst suffering and pain of starvation. I want to thank God and the United States Government for hearing our plea for hope and giving us freedom. I want to just describe very briefly my reasons for leaving North Korea.

I escaped with my two daughters from North Korea for the first time in 1998. Before defection from North Korea, my family consisted of eight people. My mother and my two month old new-born baby son died from starvation. My oldest daughter, who was 18 years old at that time, left home to find food, and never came back; to this day I do not know of her whereabouts, or what happened to her. I had another five year old son, who I had to leave at an acquaintance's home before I escaped to China. I promised my son, "If you just sleep for five nights, I will be back with rice and candy, and I will come back to get you." Afterwards, my five year old son, who was suffering from malnutrition, was kicked out of the house I had put him in, and died while waiting and crying out, 'Mommy, sister! When are you coming back . . . " He cried and cried and died in a grass field; this news was delivered to me by someone I had hired to go and bring my son to China.

My husband was arrested and sent to jail for the crime of crossing the Tumen River and going to China and bringing back a sack of rice, when what he had done was simply to go to China to find food for his children and save them, who had slowly over time grown weaker and weaker from starvation. He died while incarcerated in prison, from the severe punishment he received. Afterwards, my family was labeled as 'anti-state' traitors, for having crossed over to China, and the North Korean police and the "bowibu" (National Security Agency) agents came to look for us in our countryside village home. They came to kick us out of the village, for me to take the remaining family members and move away to another place. Our family had devoted ourselves to the Party and to the Dear Leader, but contrary to the police in the United States, instead of protecting the citizens, the North Korean police threatened to burn down our house if we did not move out. I could no longer beg for help or for mercy. I decided right then and there. Rather than staying put and starving to death, even if we die trying to go find our way to freedom, I decided to seek out freedom! My one sole wish was to feed my children just one meal of while rice, and decided that I would never suffer from starvation or be unfairly mistreated and therefore took my seven year old daughter who was malnourished and was not growing up properly, put her in a sack and carried her, and held my older daughter's hand and leaned on one another and crossed the waist-high currents of the Tumen River and safely escaped from North Korea.

After escaping to China and living in fear for almost ten years, during that period we were forcibly repatriated four times. During one of those forced repatriations, I would just like to share about my experience from the time I was forcibly repatriated during the summer of 2003.

First of all, once a North Korean defector was handed over by the Chinese police to the North Korean "bowibu", one had to become an animal, and secondly, the defectors who are repatriated are ordered by the North Korea guards that "You are all dogs from now on, so therefore lower your head and move around by only looking at the ground." The prisoners are handcuffed and chained to one another, and if the slightest noise is made, the prisoners are beaten with rifle butts. After the interrogation is finished at the "bowibu", the prisoners are taken to a reform labor camp. Where I was sent, we were forced to work from 5 in the morning until late at night, and after dragging our dead-tired bodies back from work we were given only a fist-size corn-riceball to eat, and until 11pm in the evening we were required to participate in self-reflection and self-criticism group meetings. We would then spend the rest of the night sitting in front of one another and picking off the ticks and lice from our clothes and our hair, and then sleep for a few hours, and then wake up early in the morning to the wakeup call and then get dragged out for more labor.

These punishments are repeated for as long as six months, and like my husband who died from malnutrition and starvation and the women prisoners who collapsed from fatigue and could not get up again, women and men alike had to carry heavy logs up to the mountainside and if a prisoner became injured there was no recourse for medicine or medical care. In the wintertime, there were no proper footwear, so pieces of cloth and strings would be used to cover up the feet and while working in the snow many would come down with frostbite, but we could not stop work and had to continue working, and also continue to work the following day. Sometimes the men had to shovel human waste with their own bare hands. The women prisoners would then carry the human waste mixed with dirt on their back and carry the load onto the fields. So for the crime of going to China for only wanting to live and not die from starvation, North Korean refugees who are repatriated by China become prisoners and end up suffering under crushing labor doing construction work or coal mining work, and become sick or injured, or worse, suffer in misery and pain and die while working under horrendous conditions; the wretched and poor North Korean refugees continue to suffer like this and the misery is never-ending.

For the crime of betraying the nation, in the "bowibu" prisons the North Korean refugee men who were forcibly repatriated were beaten with steel pipes, and countless people died from the beatings inflicted on them where arms and legs were broken. I myself was beaten in the head for the crime of having gone over to China, and I was beaten so severely that my skull still has pieces of bone embedded in my head. Besides this injury, because I was beaten so severely and punched around so much my eyes became swollen, and one of my ear drums ruptured, and to his day, I am hard of hearing in one ear. While we were suffering from thirst there was no water to drink, and the prisoners would end up drinking foul water from water tanks or wells, and contract dysentery and die without any care or treatment given to them.

North Korean refugees, if they are miraculously able to survive and released from prison or from the reform labor camps, will attempt to escape from North Korea even if it means death if caught again. Through this Hearing today I earnestly plead and beg of you. Refugees of other countries have been accepted in the U.S. numbering in the tens of thousands of people, but after the North Korean Human Rights Act passed in 2004, only about 130 North Korean refugees have been granted asylum in the United States.

These defectors, who have been separated from their parents, separated from their children—these defectors who have no place to go—these North Korean refugees who are shuddering in fear in China right now, are desiring freedom in the free world, whether it be South Korea or the United States, and desire to be rescued and accepted into freedom. Please help us North Korean refugees.

Thank you.

PREPARED STATEMENT OF JINHYE JO

MARCH 5, 2012

Hello my name is Jinhye Jo and I am a North Korean defector.

I want to first extend my greeting of deep appreciation to God, the United States Government, and the American people for allowing me the freedom to speak before you at this place, and also for the fact that I am living in America, a place which is like heaven to me. In North Korea one could not dream of going to Pyongyang freely unless you were a part of the inner circle of Kim Jong Il. However I am now living in the Washington, D.C. area, the capital of the United States, and I am here today to make an earnest request.

With a desire to fill our hungry stomachs, we escaped to China to seek the freedom that my mother spoke of. However, what awaited us were the Chinese police and security officials who were obsessed with searching for and arresting North Korean defectors, and human traffickers who did not see a mother of two children but rather a source of money-making. My sister and I were young and naive and were just so glad to be able to eat white rice, but we always lived in fear that one morning when we woke up our mother would be taken somewhere to be sold, or that she would abandon us and leave us. By chance I happened to find God and became a Christian at a small countryside church, and through the grace of God and his protection, even though I was forcibly repatriated four times to North Korea, I did not die from beatings, I did not die from starvation, and I was able to survive and live.

The North Korean "bowibu", or National Security Agency officials, strip search the defector women who are sent back, searching every article of clothing to look for hidden money. If nothing of value is found among the clothing, the prisoners who are standing are told to put their hands on their head and forced to sit and stand up repeatedly until they collapse from exhaustion, and if they do collapse, they are relentlessly slapped. An elderly grandmother who was 65 years old and next to me in the interrogation cell said she could not move any further, and she was immediately and mercilessly slapped and beaten, while another young girl and I had our heads bashed against the wall repeatedly. After the interrogation was over and while in transit to the prison cells, one of the prisoners had talked back to the security guard and we were then mercilessly kicked by the guard, who was wearing boots. We were placed in cells that were crawling with insects, and while trying to sleep at night, because the space was so limited, we literally had to sleep on top of other prisoners.

As a woman it is hard for me to describe what I saw and experienced, but I want to speak out today with courage for the countless North Korean refugees who have suffered under North Korea's evil and its violation of human rights. North Korean refugees swallow money wrapped in plastic when escaping to China. During arrest by the Chinese authorities and forced repatriation to North Korea and going to a prison, the money that is expelled naturally through defecation is peeled of its soiled plastic and swallowed again. Another way of hiding money for women is to hide the money in the womb or, in the anus. There was an incident at the "bowibu" facility in Sinuiju, North Korea where a 16 year old girl's hymen ruptured and she was hemorrhaging blood. The "bowibu" agent used a rubber glove to check for money or contraband in her vagina and due to the reckless searching the agent had ruptured her hymen. In their quest to search for money and rob the prisoners, they stopped at nothing, using all kinds of methods and means to do so. A lot of the women prisoners also attempted to give the money they took pains to hide to the security agents with the hope of being shown leniency or being let go.

I remember vividly what happened to a North Korean refugee woman who was pregnant with a baby conceived with a Chinese man, who was repatriated. The head "bowibu" security agent cussed profanities at her, yelling at this woman that she was a "bitch who carried Chinese seed". He then proceeded to torture and beat her with steel hooks by hitting her on the side and the head, and forcing her to sit and stand repeated for five hundred times, until she collapsed. The North Korean agents continue to pour out obscenities at the woman lying on the floor, and after they picked her up and sat her down on the floor, the agents then beat her in the head with a wooden block and caused her nose to bleed, and her blood splattered all around her in the interrogation room. I saw this with my own eyes. Besides this one example, there were situations where we were bitten by bugs and we suffered from inflammation; when the temperature got so cold and some prisoners were crying out in pain from frostbitten feet, the security guards would punish everyone in the cell.

When my family was repatriated for the last time, my mother was hauled to be tortured. Hearing our mother's blood-curdling screams, my sister and I froze instantly with fear, as if our hearts stopped. The head "bowibu" agent began to torment and scare us by saying that if we told the truth, our mother would not be hit. Despite this we didn't dare open our mouths; he grabbed our heads by our hair and began hitting us. The pain that was inflicted on us was so bad we could not lay our head down properly to sleep for about two weeks.

Another form of punishment and torture I received in the interrogation room was where I was forced to kneel down and a wooden plank was placed between my thighs and between my bent legs; every time I answered "NO" to a question I was kicked and that would cause me to bowl over. The plank that was placed was tremendously painful, and this was one way that I was tortured. Other forms of beatings and torture that I received after being forcibly repatriated by the Chinese authorities were in one instance, where I was forced to stand on tip-toes and then mercilessly kicked and beaten; kicked and beaten to unconsciousness while forced to kneel, and then the security agents would wake me up with water splashed from an ashtray. My own mother was beaten in the head with a log so harshly, pieces of her skull cracked, and because she was also severely beaten with fists by the security agents, her eardrum ruptured and to this day she is hard of hearing in one ear. All these methods of severe and cruel punishment were to try to find out whether the North Korean refugees had attempted to eventually escape to South Korea, or whether they had attended church or come into contact with Christians while in China. Our family I believe was miraculously saved through God's special grace and mercy. I also believe that God saved me so that I would be able to tell the world the plight of the North Korean people's unfair suffering, and the worst modern-day evil that is going on right now.

When I think of the almost three dozen North Korean refugees who will be experiencing torture and fear on a far worse scale than what I went through, I am filled with dread and fear, and my heart aches so much. The North Korean regime under Kim Jong Un has declared that any North Korean that attempts to escape during the mourning period for Kim Jong Il will be dealt with most severely, and these refugees who have embarrassed the regime and sought the world's attention to save them, will surely be punished to three generations and be given the harshest sentence, if they are repatriated by China.

I sincerely and earnestly request all of you here today, and for those throughout the world who will hear this Hearing, that the good fortune and privilege we have now of living in freedom, will become a reality for those more than 30 North Korean refugees currently being held by China, only through your combined attention and effort. I sincerely and earnestly request that you will help save the precious lives of these more than 30 North Korean refugees, lives that are more precious than anything in this world, through talking with the Government of China, even as they are pushing down people who are drowning and reaching out their hands to be rescued.

China & North Korea, Stop Killing People!!!

Thank you.

————

Prepared Statement of T. Kumar

March 5, 2012

Thank you Mr. Chairman and member of the Congressional-Executive Commission on China, Amnesty International is pleased to testify at this important hearing on China's repatriation of North Korean refugees.

Amnesty International have been closely monitoring the plight of North Korean refugees in China for over a decade and have published reports on the treatment of North Korean refugees by the Chinese authorities, reasons why North Koreans flee their country and the abuses faced by North Korean refugees forcibly returned to North Korea.

Despite China being a Permanent Member of the UN Security Council and a state party to the UN Refugee Convention; with respect to North Korean border-crossers residing without legal documentation, China completely disregards its commitments to and obligations under the international system. China denies these North Koreans the enjoyment of full protection of their human rights and refugee rights in China.

Chinese authorities forcibly returns North Korean border-crossers back to North Korea where they face risk to their lives. By its actions, it intimidates North Korean border-crossers and those who are helping them in China. China refuses to give access to the UN refugee agency, the UN High Commissioner for Refugees (UNHCR).

Those individuals apprehended by Chinese border police and North Korean authorities in China are reportedly detained in China for several days and then forcibly returned to their country where they are at risk of punishment including arbitrary detention, forced labor, and in some cases, the death penalty for leaving the country without authorization.

BACKGROUND

The acute food shortages in North Korea since the early 1990s have forced tens of thousands of people to cross the border "illegally" into China's north-eastern provinces. According to NGOs, journalists and aid workers who have visited the region, thousands of North Koreans are currently residing in border areas.

Amnesty International believes that all North Korean in China are entitled to refugee status because of threat of human rights violations if they were to be returned to North Korea against their will.

The North Korean authorities criminalize the act of leaving the country without State approval and consider it a political offence, even though the motive for leaving the country may simply be one of survival. This along with harsh punishments faced by those who are returned would indicate that almost all North Korean who flee are at risk of facing severe abuses once returned.

Their plight is made even more precarious by reports suggesting a January 2012 announcement by the North Korean authorities condemning border-crossers and threatening them with severe punishments. The announcement comes at a time when North Korea's leadership is in transition.

Amnesty International is concerned that this reported denouncement of border-crossers could signal a crackdown against any potential dissent at this key time in North Korea. Additionally, those who are forcibly returned now may face even harsher punishment than usual.

North Korean authorities refuse to recognize or grant access to international human rights monitors, including Amnesty International and the UN Special Rapporteur on the situation of human rights in the Democratic People's Republic of Korea (North Korea).

REPATRIATION AND THE PRINCIPLE OF NON-REFOULEMENT

Article 33 (1) of the 1951 Convention relating to the Status of Refugees, states that:

> No Contracting State shall expel or return ('refouler') a refugee in any manner whatsoever to the frontiers of territories where his life or freedom would be threatened on account of his race, religion, nationality, membership of a particular social group or political opinion.

International law prohibits the forcible return, either directly or indirectly, of any individuals to a country where they are at risk of persecution, torture or other ill-treatment, or death.

CHINA-NORTH KOREA BILATERAL AGREEMENT

According to a White Paper published by the South Korean think-tank KINU in 2011, "North Korea's State Safety Protection Agency and China's Public Safety Agency have been enforcing strict controls over the movement of their citizens across the border based on the "Bilateral Agreement on Mutual Cooperation for the Maintenance of State Safety and Social Order" (July 1998).

PLIGHT OF NORTH KOREAN REFUGEES IN CHINA

Despite significant risks, thousands of North Koreans illegally cross the border into China every year. China considers all undocumented North Koreans to be economic migrants, rather than as asylum seekers, and forcibly returns them to North Korea if they are caught.

North Koreans residing "illegally" in China live in appalling conditions and are vulnerable to physical, emotional and sexual exploitation. North Koreans living in China live in constant fear of being caught detained by Chinese authorities and forcibly returned to China.

North Korean border-crossers in China are in a very precarious situation. Some find shelter in villages and farms where they are supported by China's ethnic Korean community and ethnic Chinese people, several work in the service industry but are vulnerable to exploitation and discrimination given their lack of legal status to reside in China. Others are forced into begging.

Surveillance and checking for "illegal" North Koreans in China have intensified and there have been even reports of North Korean authorities crossing the border to "detain" some North Korean border-crossers and "abduct" them back to North Korea.

North Koreans in China are denied their right to seek and enjoy asylum from persecution. Although China is a party to the Refugee Convention, NGOs and other advocates for North Korean asylum-seekers in China say that it is virtually impossible for North Koreans to access refugee determination procedures with UNHCR, or be afforded protection as a group.

According to several reports Amnesty International has received from NGOs and contacts in Japan, South Korea, Europe and the USA, China regularly returns North Koreans back to their country of origin without giving them the opportunity to make a claim for asylum and without making an objective and informed decision that the North Koreans would be protected against serious human rights abuses in North Korea.

The Government of China have on occasion also arrested and imprisoned NGO activists—most of whom are South Korean or Japanese nationals—and others who have been attempting to help North Koreans to leave China and reach South Korea.

WHAT HAPPENS TO THE NORTH KOREAN BORDER-CROSSERS REPATRIATED FROM CHINA?

Detention

According to testimonies from North Korean border-crossers, all those forcibly repatriated from China are detained and interrogated in detention centers or police stations operated by the National Security Agency or the People's Safety Agency. The detainees are often subjected to torture.

There appear to be several factors that influence the severity of the punishment meted out to North Koreans who have been forcibly returned from China. After the interrogation, "depending on the number of times the person had been in China, depending on their background (if the person had been serving in the military or was a government official, then the interrogation and sentencing appear to be more severe) and if the authorities have been convinced that the detainees are not 'politically dangerous', they are sent to a village unit labor camp, where they spend between three months and three years in forced labor.

If the North Korean border-crossers are considered to be politically sensitive such as serving or retired government officials or military personnel, they are at risk of being sent to a political prison camp.

North Korean border-crossers who have been in touch with South Korean nationals or with religious groups while in China are at great risk of being sent to political prison camps.

Execution

In 2011, Amnesty International reported testimonies of former detainees at political prison camp 15 at Yodok, that prisoners are forced to work in conditions approaching slavery and are frequently subjected to torture and other cruel, inhuman, or degrading treatment. All those interviewed had witnessed public executions.

WOMEN

Women suffer particularly because of the social roles ascribed to them. Women are generally responsible for finding food for their families, and in times of scarcity often have the last call on food within a household. Many have been forced to roam the countryside in search of food, medicine and other daily necessities. A large proportion of those crossing the border into China for these purposes are women.

In its 2003 concluding observations on North Korea, the Committee on Economic, Social and Cultural Rights expressed its concern about the: "persistence of traditional attitudes and practices prevailing . . . with regard to women that negatively affect their enjoyment of economic, social and cultural rights. The Committee is concerned about the lack of domestic legislation on non-discrimination against women and about the persistence of de facto inequality . . ."

Information received by Amnesty International indicates that a growing number of women have been forced to turn to prostitution to feed themselves and their hungry families.

Amnesty International has also documented an increase in the number of North Korean women being trafficked to China by Chinese bride traffickers where they are sold on to ethnic Korean farmers of Chinese nationality who have difficulty finding wives.

CHILDREN

The Committee on Rights of the Child expressed concern in June 2004 at reports of North Korean street children in Chinese border towns. It was also deeply concerned at reports that children (and their families) returning or forcibly returned back to North Korea were considered by the North Korea government not as victims but as perpetrators of a crime.

NORTH KOREAN LAW

North Koreans who flee their country are usually considered by their government to be traitors and/or criminals if they leave North Korea without official permission. Article 47 of the 1987 North Korean Criminal Code states that:

A citizen of the Republic who defects to a foreign country or to the enemy in betrayal of the country and the people...shall be committed to a reform institution for not less than seven years. In cases where the person commits an extremely grave concern, he or she shall be given the death penalty . . .

Article 117 states:

A person who crosses a frontier of the Republic without permission shall be committed to a reform institution for up to three years.

The North Korean law which prohibits unauthorized departure is in clear breach of the fundamental right to leave one's own country. Article 12 (2) of the International Covenant on Civil and Political Rights (ICCPR), to which North Korea is a state party, states that "(e)veryone shall be free to leave any country, including his own."

North Koreans who "illegally" cross or help others in crossing the North Korean border face heavy penalties. Under Article 117 of the Criminal Code, a person who illegally crosses "a frontier of the Republic" faces a sentence of up to three years in a kwalliso (a political prison camp).

In a 2006 media briefing, "North Korea: Human rights concerns", Amnesty International stated that the large numbers of North Korean border-crossers being forcibly repatriated back from China have caused the North Korean government to ease sentences and change the penal code. The 1999 version of the penal code distinguished between "unlawful border crossing" and crossing "with the intent to overturn the Republic".

The 2004 revision of the North Korean penal code further distinguishes between "crossing" and "frequent crossings". According to the latter version, "frequent crossing" of the border without permission is a criminal act punishable by up to two years in labor camps (three years in the 1999 version).

Acts of treason, such as "surrendering, changing allegiance, [and] handing over confidential information", are punishable by five to ten years of hard labor, or ten years to life in more serious cases.

RECOMMENDATIONS

The Government of China should:

• Stop immediately all operations by Chinese and the North Korean officials aimed at apprehending and intimidating North Korean border-crossers and those who are helping them in China.

• Respect its obligations under international human rights and refugee law. This includes protecting the fundamental human rights of all North Koreans on its territory. In particular, asylum-seekers should have access to a fair, satisfactory and individual refugee status determination procedure.

• North Korean asylum-seekers should be given access to the UNHCR so that their claims for protection can be independently and impartially assessed. Persons found to be refugees under a fair and satisfactory procedure should have access to effective respect for their fundamental human rights, including their economic, social and cultural rights.

• In accordance with the customary norm of non-refoulement and its obligations under the Convention against Torture and the Refugee Convention, the Government of China should not forcibly return any North Korean to North Korea who may be subject to serious human rights abuses, including imprisonment, torture, execution or other punishment inflicted for leaving the country without authorization.

• Immediately end all bilateral re-admission agreements [with North Korea] which deny asylum-seekers and refugees access to a fair and satisfactory asylum-procedure and effective and durable protection from refoulement.

• Lift restrictions on access to the border areas with North Korea for the UNHCR, independent human rights monitors and other independent observers, agencies and organizations.

The Government of North Korea should:

• Respect the right to freedom of movement for all North Koreans, especially to ensure that they have adequate access to food. The North Korean government should not punish individuals whose only crime is to try and feed their family.

• The North Korean government should, especially, refrain from punishing its citizens who have moved to other countries, in particular for humanitarian reasons, and refrain from treating their departure as criminal or even as treason leading to punishments of imprisonment, inhuman or degrading treatment or the death penalty.

• Stop all executions.

• Respect the right of access to information—including by allowing independent news media to publish and broadcast and by granting free and unimpeded access to media outlets—so that ordinary people are aware of the gravity of the food situation and of their human rights.

• Allow independent international human rights monitors.

The Government of the United States should:

(1) Raise North Korean refugee protection issues in all its meetings with the Chinese Government, including during the annual Security and Economic Dialogue and Human Rights Dialogue.

(2) Ensure that the Government of China respects its obligations under international law, including respecting the fundamental principle of non-refoulement, by not forcibly repatriating North Korean Refugees.

(3) Urge the Chinese Government to stop arresting and intimidating North Korean refugees.

(4) Urge the Chinese Government to fulfill its obligations under the 1951 Convention relating to the Status of Refugees, including respect for the right of North Koreans to seek and enjoy asylum.

(5) Urge the North Korean Government not to punish North Korean refugees brought back to North Korea.

(6) Help resettle North Korean refugees.

Thank you for inviting Amnesty International to testify in this hearing.

———

PREPARED STATEMENT OF GREG SCARLATOIU

MARCH 5, 2012

Good afternoon, Chairman Smith, Cochairman Brown, and members of the Commission. On behalf of the Committee for Human Rights in North Korea, thank you for inviting me to speak with you at this hearing today. Our Committee considers it essential to draw attention to the case of 30 to 40 North Koreans who have been arrested by China and who now risk being forcibly returned to North Korea where they most assuredly will be subjected to severe punishment in violation of international refugee and human rights law. The fundamental right to leave a country, to seek asylum abroad and not to be forcibly returned to conditions of danger are internationally recognized rights which China and North Korea must be obliged to respect.

Mr. Chair, the Committee for Human Rights in North Korea is a Washington DC-based non-governmental organization, established in 2001. Our Committee's main statement has been prepared by Chair Roberta Cohen, who was unable to be here today. I will draw upon that statement in my opening remarks.

Over the past two decades, considerable numbers of North Koreans have risked their lives to cross the border into China. They have done so because of starvation, economic deprivation or political persecution. It is estimated that there are thousands or tens of thousands in China today. Most are vulnerable to forced returns where they will face persecution and punishment because leaving North Korea without permission is a criminal offense. Yet to China, all North Koreans are economic migrants, and over the years, it has forcibly returned tens of thousands to conditions of danger. According to the testimonies and reports received by the Committee for Human Rights, the North Koreans returned to their country endure cruel and inhuman punishment including beatings, torture, detention, forced labor, sexual violence, and in the case of women suspected of become pregnant in China, forced abortions or infanticide. Some have even been executed.

We therefore submit that North Koreans in China merit international refugee protection for the following reasons: First, a definite number of those who cross the border may do so out of a well founded fear of persecution on political, social or religious grounds that would accord with the 1951 Refugee Convention. Second, the reasons why these North Koreans flee to China go beyond the economic realm. Those who cross the border into China for reasons of economic deprivation are often from poorer classes, without access to the food and material benefits enjoyed by the privileged political elite. Subject to North Korea's *songbun* classification system, their quest for economic survival may be based on political persecution. Examining such cases in a refugee determination process might establish that certain numbers crossing into China for economic survival merit refugee status. Third, and by far the most compelling argument why North Koreans should not be forcibly returned is that most if not all fit the category of refugees sur place. As defined by the UN High Commissioner for Refugees (UNHCR), refugees sur place are persons who might not have been refugees when they left their country but who become refugees at a later date because they have a valid fear of persecution upon return. North Koreans who leave their country for reasons including economic motives have valid reasons for fearing persecution and punishment upon return. Accordingly, UNHCR has urged China not to forcibly return North Koreans and has proposed a special humanitarian status for them so that they can obtain temporary documentation and access to services and not be repatriated.

China, however, has refused to allow UNHCR access to North Koreans in border areas where it could set up a screening process. It considers itself bound by an agreement it made with North Korea in 1986 obliging both countries to prevent "illegal border crossings," which replaced an earlier 1960 agreement. It also stands by its local law in Jilin province (1993) which requires the return of North Koreans who enter illegally. Both documents stand in violation of China's obligations under the 1951 Refugee Convention (which it signed in 1982), its membership in UNHCR's Executive Committee (EXCOM), and the human rights agreements it has ratified. These include the Convention against Torture, which prohibits the return of persons to states where they could be subjected to torture, and the Convention on the Rights of the Child, which prohibits the return of unaccompanied children to countries where they could be irreparably harmed.

It is reported that some local Chinese officials have at times provided documents to North Korean women married to Han Chinese, which allows them and their children some form of protection and access to medical and educational services. Such practices should be encouraged but they are not Chinese policy or law. Most North Koreans in China have no rights and are vulnerable to exploitation, forced marriages and trafficking as well as to forced returns where they will face persecution and punishment. Our Committee's report *Lives for Sale: Personal Accounts of Women Fleeing North Korea to China,* 2010, documents the experiences of North Korean women in China and the extreme lack of protection for them.

To encourage China to fulfill its international obligations to North Koreans on its territory, our Committee puts forward the following recommendations:

First, the United States Congress should consider additional hearings on the plight of North Koreans who cross into China to keep a spotlight on the issue and try to avert forced repatriations to conditions of danger.

Second, members of Congress should consider supporting the efforts of the Parliamentary Forum for Democracy, established in 2010, so that joint inter-parliamentary efforts can be mobilized in a number of countries on behalf of the North Koreans in danger in China.

Third, the United States should encourage UNHCR to raise its profile on this issue. It further should lend its full support to UNHCR's appeals and proposals to China and mobilize other governments to do likewise in order to make sure that the provisions of the 1951 Refugee Convention are upheld and the work of this important UN agency enhanced.

Fourth, together with other concerned governments, the United States should give priority to raising the forced repatriation of North Koreans with Chinese officials but in the absence of a response, should bring the issue before international refugee and human rights fora. UNHCR's Executive Committee as well as the UN Human Rights Council and General Assembly of the United Nations should all be expected to call on China by name to carry out its obligations under refugee and human rights law and enact legislation to codify these obligations so that North Koreans will not be expelled if their lives or freedom are in danger.

Fifth, the United States should consider promoting a multilateral approach to the problem of North Koreans leaving their country. Their exodus affects more than China. It concerns South Korea most notably, whose Constitution offers citizenship to North Koreans. Countries in East and Southeast Asia, East and West Europe as well as Mongolia and the United States are also affected. Together with UNHCR, a multilateral approach should be designed that finds solutions for North Koreans based on principles of non-refoulement and human rights and humanitarian protection. International burden sharing has been introduced for other refugee populations and could be developed here.

Sixth, the United States should consider ways to enhance its readiness to increase the number of North Korean refugees and asylum seekers admitted to this country. Other countries should be encouraged as well to take in more North Korean refugees and asylum seekers until such time as they no longer face persecution and punishment in their country.

Thank you, Mr. Chairman, and members of the Commission. I look forward to answering any questions you might have.

———

PREPARED STATEMENT OF HON. CHRIS SMITH, A U.S. REPRESENTATIVE FROM NEW JERSEY; CHAIRMAN, CONGRESSIONAL-EXECUTIVE COMMISSION ON CHINA

CHINA'S FORCED REPATRIATION OF NORTH KOREAN REFUGEES VIOLATES INTERNATIONAL LAW

MARCH 5, 2012

Dozens of North Koreans are today at imminent risk of persecution, torture—even execution—owing to China's decision to forcibly repatriate them in stark violation of both the spirit and the letter of the 1951 Refugee Convention and 1967 Protocol to which China has acceded.

The international community—especially the United Nations, the Obama Administration and the US Congress—must insist that China at long last honor its treaty obligations, end its egregious practice of systematic refoulement, or be exposed as hypocrites

Article 33 of the Convention and Protocol Relating to the Status of Refugees couldn't be more clear:

> Prohibition of Explusion or Return ("Refoulement"): No Contracting State shall expel or return ("refouler") a refugee in any manner whatsoever to the frontiers of territories where his life or freedom would be threatened on account of his race, religion, nationality, membership of a particular social group or political opinion.

Today's hearing underscores an emergency that begs an immediate remedy. Lives are at risk. The North Korean refugees—disproportionately women—face death or severe sexual abuse and torture unless they get immediate protection. China has a duty to protect.

In recent weeks we have had learned that Chinese authorities have reportedly detained dozens—perhaps more than 40—North Korean refugees. North Korea's leader, Kim Jong-un, has threatened to "exterminate three generations" or any family with a member caught defecting from North Korea during the 100-day mourning period for the late Kim Jong-il. I believe him.

It's unclear whether or not the Obama Administration's food aid to North Korea—some 240,000 metric tons per year—contains any conditions or links to the refugees. It should.

Forced repatriation by China of North Koreans isn't new. But that doesn't make what is about to happen to dozens of new victims any less offensive.

According to testimony submitted today by Roberta Cohen, Chair of the Committee for Human Right in North Korea and Non-Resident Senior Fellow at the Brookings Institution, "China has forcibly returned tens of thousands over the past two decades. Most if not all have been punished in North Korea and according to the testimonies and reports received by the Committee for Human Rights, the punishment has included beatings, torture, detention, forced labor, sexual violence, and in the case of women suspected of become pregnant in China, forced abortions or infanticide."

For the record, since 2005 alone, I have chaired four congressional human rights hearings that focused in whole or in part on the plight of North Korean refugees and China's ongoing violations of international law. They include:

- Human Rights in North Korea: Challenges and Opportunities (Sept. 20, 2011)
  http://foreignaffairs.house.gov/112/68443.pdf

- North Korea: Human Rights Update and International Abduction Issues (April 27, 2006)
  http://democrats.foreignaffairs.house.gov/archives/109/27228.pdf

- Lifting the Veil: Getting the Refugees Out, Getting Our Message In: An Update on the Implementation of the North Korean Human Rights Act (Oct. 27, 2005)
  http://democrats.foreignaffairs.house.gov/archives/109/24202.pdf

- The North Korean Human Rights Act of 2004: Issues and Implications (April 28, 2005)
  http://democrats.foreignaffairs.house.gov/archives/109/20919.pdf

The Chinese government claims that the North Korean refugees are "illegal economic migrants"—not refugees. Furthermore, the Chinese government continues its policy of repatriating North Koreans in China according to a bilateral repatriation agreement that requires it return all border crossers. As we will hear today, in doing so, China is in clear violation of its obligations under the 1951 Convention Relating to the Status of Refugees and its 1967 Protocol, to which China has acceded. Under international law and standards, these detained refugees are entitled to protection if there is well-founded reason to believe that they will be persecuted upon return. As our witnesses will attest, we know what the detained refugees face. There are documented accounts, as well as strong evidence. We know that persecution exists.

North Korea is certainly at fault. It must also be stated that China has contributed to the humanitarian crisis through its policy of gendercide—the killing of baby girls by forced abortion of infanticide. China's one-child policy has led to the worst gender disparity in any nation in history, and that is directly connected to the issue we probe today. According to the 2011 CECC Annual Report, NGOs and researchers estimate that as many as 70 percent of the North Korean refugees in China are women. And some researchers have estimated that 9 out of every 10 North Korean women in China are trafficked. There is a high demand for wives in northeastern China where severe sex ratio imbalances have fueled the trafficking of North Korean women for commercial sexual exploitation and forced marriage.

Our focus today is China's role and responsibility in solving this immediate problem. At this time, we call on China to uphold its international obligations and take immediate steps to end this cruel policy of sending North Koreans back to persecution or death. China must conform to international norms and allow these refugees safe passage to the Republic of Korea, or grant them immediate asylum. And, we ask that the Chinese government take all necessary steps to meet the requirements of the Convention Relating to the Status of Refugees and its Protocol.

I welcome and thank all of our witnesses. It is an extraordinary honor to welcome Ms. Han Song-hwa and her daughter Jo Jin-hye, former North Korean refugees who are here to share their personal accounts of detention, hardship and loss. I am sure that their reflections and observations will deepen our understanding of this issue and strengthen our insistence that China immediately address this crisis.

SUBMISSION FOR THE RECORD

WRITTEN STATEMENT OF ROBERTA COHEN, CHAIR, COMMITTEE FOR HUMAN RIGHTS IN NORTH KOREA, AND NON-RESIDENT SENIOR FELLOW, THE BROOKINGS INSTITUTION, ON CHINA'S REPATRIATION OF NORTH KOREAN REFUGEES

MARCH 5, 2012

On behalf of the Committee for Human Rights in North Korea, I would like to express great appreciation to Congressman Christopher Smith and Senator Sherrod Brown for holding this hearing today to highlight the case of an estimated 30 to 40 North Koreans who fled into China and now risk being forcibly returned to North Korea where they will most assuredly be severely punished. We consider it essential to defend the fundamental rights of North Koreans to leave their country and seek asylum abroad and to call upon China to stop its forcible repatriation of North Koreans and provide them with the needed human rights and humanitarian protection to which they are entitled. The right to leave a country, to seek asylum abroad and not to be forcibly returned to conditions of danger are internationally recognized rights which North Korea and China, like all other countries, are obliged to respect.

This particular case of North Koreans has captured regional and international attention. South Korean President Lee Myung Bak has spoken out publicly against the return of the North Koreans and National Assembly woman Park Sun Young has undertaken a hunger strike in front of the Chinese Embassy in Seoul. The Parliamentary Forum for Democracy encompassing 18 countries has urged its members to raise the matter with their governments.

The case, however, is situated at the tip of the iceberg. According to the State Department's Human Rights Report (2010), there may be thousands or tens of thousands of North Koreans hiding in China. Although China does allow large numbers of North Koreans to reside illegally in its country, they have no rights and China has forcibly returned tens of thousands over the past two decades. Most if not all have been punished in North Korea and according to the testimonies and reports received by the Committee for Human Rights, the punishment has included beatings, torture, detention, forced labor, sexual violence, and in the case of women suspected of become pregnant in China, forced abortions or infanticide.

Stringent punishment in particular has been meted out to North Koreans who have associated abroad with foreigners (i.e., missionaries, aid workers or journalists) or have sought political asylum or tried to obtain entry into South Korea. The North Koreans currently arrested and threatened with return are therefore likely to suffer severe punishment should they be repatriated. Some might even face execution; the North Korean Ministry of Public Security issued a decree in 2010 making the crime of defection a "crime of treachery against the nation."

The Committee for Human Rights in North Korea, a Washington DC-based nongovernmental organization, established in 2001, has published three in-depth reports on the precarious plight of North Koreans in China and the cruel and inhuman practice of forcibly sending them back to one of the world's most oppressive regimes. The first, *The North Korean Refugee Crisis: Human Rights and International Response* (2006), edited by Stephan Haggard and Marcus Noland, establishes that most if not all North Koreans in China merit a prima facie claim to refugee or refugee sur place status. The second, *Lives for Sale: Personal Accounts of Women Fleeing North Korea to China* (2010) calls upon China to set up a screening process with the UN High Commissioner for Refugees (UNHCR) to determine the status of North Koreans and ensure they are not forcibly returned. The third, to be published in April, *Hidden Gulag* second edition, by David Hawk, presents the harrowing testimony of scores of North Koreans severely punished after being returned to North Korea.

REASONS NORTH KOREANS IN CHINA SHOULD BE CONSIDERED REFUGEES

Although China claims that North Koreans in its country are economic migrants subject to deportation, we submit that North Koreans in China should merit international refugee protection for the following reasons:

First, a definite number of those who cross the border can be expected to do so out of a well founded fear of persecution on political, social or religious grounds. It is well known that in their own country North Koreans suffer persecution if they express or even appear to hold political views unacceptable to the authorities, listen to foreign broadcasts, watch South Korean DVDs, practice their own religious beliefs, or try to leave the country. Some 200,000 are incarcerated in labor camps and other penal facilities on political grounds. Moreover, North Koreans imprisoned for having gone to China for food or employment often try, once released, to leave again. Some conclude they will always be under suspicion, surveillance and persecution in North Korea and therefore cross the border once again, this time seeking political refuge, ultimately in South Korea.

Because China has no refugee adjudication process to determine who is a refugee and the UN High Commissioner for Refugees (UNHCR) has no access to North Koreans at the border, it has not been possible to ascertain how many North Koreans are seeking asylum because of a well-founded fear of political or other persecution. But those who cross the border because of political, religious or social persecution will no doubt fit the definition of refugee under the 1951 Convention Relating to the Status of Refugees and its 1967 Protocol.[1]

Second, those who cross the border into China for reasons of economic deprivation, probably the majority, may also qualify as refugees if they have been compelled to leave North Korea because of government economic policies that could be shown to be tantamount to political persecution. These North Koreans are not part of the privileged political elite and therefore have insufficient access to food and material supplies. In times of economic hardship in particular, food is distributed by the government first to the army and Party based on political loyalty whereas many of the North Koreans crossing into China during periods of famine are from the "impure," "wavering" or "hostile" classes, which are the poor, deprived lower classes, designated as such under North Korea's *songbun* caste system.[2] Their quest for economic survival could therefore be based on political discrimination and persecution. Examining such cases in a refugee determination process might establish that certain numbers of North Koreans crossing into China for economic survival merit refugee status under the 1951 Convention.

Third, and by far the most compelling argument why North Koreans should not be forcibly returned is that most if not all fit the category of refugees sur place. As defined by UNHCR, refugees sur place are persons who might not have been refugees when they left their country but who become refugees "at a later date" because they have a valid fear of persecution upon return. North Koreans who leave their country because of economic reasons have valid reasons for fearing persecution and punishment upon return. Their government after all deems it a criminal offense to leave the country without permission and punishes persons who are returned, or even who return voluntarily. North Koreans in China therefore could qualify as refugees sur place.

The High Commissioner for Refugees, Antonio Guterres in 2006 while on a visit to China raised the concept of refugees sur place with Chinese officials. He told them that forcibly repatriating North Koreans without any determination process and where they could be persecuted on return stands in violation of the Refugee Convention. To UNHCR since 2004, North Koreans in China without permission are deemed "persons of concern," meriting humanitarian protection.[3] It has proposed to China a special humanitarian status for North Koreans, which would enable them to obtain temporary documentation, access to services, and protection from forced return. To date, China has failed to agree to this temporary protected status.

While China has cooperated with UNHCR in making arrangements for Vietnamese and other refugees to integrate in China or resettle elsewhere, it has refused to cooperate when it comes to North Koreans. Only in cases where North Koreans have made their way to foreign embassies or consulates or the UNHCR compound in Beijing has China felt impelled to cooperate with governments or the UNHCR in facilitating their departure to South Korea or other countries. In the vast majority of cases, China considers itself bound to an agreement it made with

---

[1] Under the Convention, a person is a refugee if he or she is outside his/her country of origin because of "a well-founded fear of being persecuted" for "reasons of race, religion, nationality, membership of a particular social group or political opinion" and unable or unwilling to avail him or herself of the protection of that country. An exception is if the person has committed criminal acts (although in the case of North Korea, the term criminal would be open to discussion).

[2] See Committee for Human Rights in North Korea, *Marked for Life: Songbun, North Korea's Social Classification System,* 2012 (forthcoming).

[3] In September 2004, the High Commissioner announced before UNHCR's Executive Committee that North Koreans in China are 'persons of concern." One reason why UNHCR used this term was that it had no access to the North Koreans; another was that under the Refugee Convention, persons of dual nationality could be excluded from refugee status. (However it has been pointed out that in the case of North Koreans, not all are able to avail themselves of their right to citizenship in South Korea, some may not choose to do so, and South Korea may not take in every North Korean. The United States and other countries do not consider North Koreans ineligible for refugee status because of the dual nationality provision.)

North Korea in 1986 (the "Mutual Cooperation Protocol for the Work of Maintaining National Security and Social Order and the Border Areas"). This agreement obliges China and North Korea to prevent "illegal border crossings of residents." Chinese police as a result collaborate with North Korean police in tracking down North Koreans and forcibly returning them to North Korea without any reference to their rights under refugee or human rights law or the obligations of China under the agreements it has ratified. Implementation of this agreement sounds remarkably like the efforts made by the former Soviet Union to support the German Democratic Republic's actions to punish East Germans for trying to leave their country. It is an agreement that undermines and stands in violation of China's obligations under the 1951 Convention Relating to the Status of Refugees (which it signed in 1982), its membership in UNHCR's Executive Committee (EXCOM), which seeks to promote refugee protection, and the human rights agreements to which China has chosen to adhere. So too do China's domestic laws contradict its international refugee and human rights commitments. A local law in Jilin province (1993) requires the return of North Koreans who enter the province illegally.

China is bound not only by the Refugee Convention that prohibits non-refoulement but the Convention against Torture and Other Cruel, Inhuman or Degrading Treatment or Punishment, which China ratified in 1988. It prohibits the return of persons to states "where there are substantial grounds for believing" that they would be "subjected to torture." Indeed, the Committee against Torture (CAT), the expert body monitoring the convention's implementation, has called upon China to establish a screening process to examine whether North Koreans will face the risk of torture on return, to provide UNHCR access to all North Korean persons of concern, and to adopt legislation incorporating China's obligations under the convention, in particular with regard to deportations.

Another UN expert body, the Committee on the Rights of the Child, which monitors compliance by China and other states with the Convention on the Rights of the Child, similarly has called on China to ensure that no unaccompanied child from North Korea is returned to a country "where there are substantial grounds for believing that there is a real risk of irreparable harm to the child."

China of course has legitimate interests in wanting to control its borders. It is concerned about potential large scale outflows from North Korea and the impact of such flows on North Korea's stability. It also is said to be concerned about potential Korean nationalism in its border areas where there are historic Korean claims. But China should not become complicit in the serious human rights violations perpetrated by North Korea against its own citizens. The reports of the United Nations Secretary-General and of the Special Rapporteur on human rights in North Korea as well as the resolutions of the General Assembly, adopted by more than 100 states, have strongly criticized North Korea for its practices and called upon North Korea's "neighboring states" to cease the deportation of North Koreans because of the terrible mistreatment they are known to endure upon return.

RECOMMENDATIONS

To encourage China to fulfill its international obligations in this matter, the following recommendations are offered:

First, additional hearings should be held by the United States Congress on the plight of North Koreans who cross into China. A spotlight must be kept on the issue to seek to avert China's forced repatriation of North Koreans to situations where their lives are at risk.

Second, members of Congress should lend support to the efforts of the Parliamentary Forum for Democracy, established in 2010, so that joint inter-parliamentary efforts can be mobilized in a number of countries around the world on behalf of the North Koreans in danger in China. Such joint efforts can also offer solidarity to South Korean colleagues protesting the forced return of North Koreans.

Third, the United States should encourage UNHCR to raise its profile on this issue. It further should lend its full support to UNHCR's appeals and proposals to China and mobilize other governments to do likewise in order to make sure that the non-refoulement provision of the 1951 Refugee Convention is upheld and the work of this important UN agency enhanced. China's practices at present threaten to undermine the principles of the international refugee protection regime.

Fourth, together with other concerned governments, the United States should give priority to raising the forced repatriation of North Koreans with Chinese officials but in the absence of response, should bring the issue before international refugee and human rights fora. UNHCR's Executive Committee as well as the UN Human Rights Council and General Assembly of the United Nations should all be expected to call on China by name to carry out its obligations under refugee and human rights law and enact legislation to codify these obligations so that North Koreans will not be expelled if their lives or freedom are in danger. Specifically, China should be called upon to adopt legislation incorporating its obligations under the Refugee Convention and international human rights agreements and to bring its existing laws into line with internationally agreed upon principles. It should be expected to call a moratorium on deportations of North Koreans until its laws and practices are brought into line with international standards and can ensure that North Koreans will not be returned to conditions of danger.

Fifth, the United States should promote a multilateral approach to the problem of North Koreans leaving their country. Their exodus affects more than China. It concerns South Korea most notably, which already houses more than 23,000 North Korean 'defectors' and whose Constitution offers citizenship to North Koreans. Countries in East and Southeast Asia, East and West Europe as well as Mongolia and the United States are also affected as they too have admitted North Korean refugees and asylum seekers. Together with UNHCR, a multilateral approach should be designed that finds solutions for North Koreans based on principles of non-refoulement and human rights and humanitarian protection. International burden sharing has been introduced for other refugee populations and should be developed here.

Sixth, the United States should make known its readiness to increase the number of North Korean refugees and asylum seekers admitted to this country.[4] Other countries should be encouraged as well to step forward and take in more North Korean refugees and asylum seekers until such time as they no longer face persecution and punishment in their country.

Thank you.

○

---

[4] See Roberta Cohen, "Admitting North Korean Refugees to the United States: Obstacles and Opportunities," *38 North,* September 20, 2011.

www.ingramcontent.com/pod-product-compliance
Lightning Source LLC
Chambersburg PA
CBHW082153290526
45794CB00008B/3273